WHAT IS RELIGIOUS LIFE?

WHAT IS RELIGIOUS LIFE?
A Critical Reappraisal

JEROME MURPHY-O'CONNOR, O.P.

With an Introduction by Sr. Kathleen Ashe O. P.

Michael Glazier, Inc.
Wilmington, Delaware

First American edition published in 1977 by

Michael Glazier, Inc.
1210-A King Street
Wilmington, DE 19801

The text of this volume first appeared in the *Supplement to Doctrine and Life,* numbers 45, 49, 50, 54, 58.

Library of Congress Catalog Number: 77-80218
ISBN: 0-89453-074-7

Printed in the United States of America.

CONTENTS

INTRODUCTION

This reappraisal of religious life by J. Murphy-O'Connor will be welcomed by all those who have yawned over high-flown pieces of rhetoric bearing no relation to the real questions facing religious today. There is neither pious claptrap nor mindless repetition of formulae here. There is rather a refreshing examination of religious life based securely on scripture and on dialogue with living and thinking members of religious communities.

The emphasis placed on community in this reappraisal springs from serious reflection on both these sources. In the wake of Vatican II religious were seeking anchors, as structures crumbled and former definitions of their form of life lost meaning. The definition offered here—religious life as essentially a life of Christian witness in community—has several advantages. First, it cuts through accidental features and historical accretions to set in sharp relief the life-giving scriptural source of religious life. Secondly, poverty, celibacy, and authority are seen in a context which clearly underscores their function of promoting, not stunting, human development; freedom, maturity, and responsible decision-making are at home in this context. Thirdly, it answers a need not only of religious and of the Church, but of the world at large for assurance that people can live in genuine community where simplicity, love, and reconciliation are manifest, and where the need of one becomes the obligation of all. It is interesting to note in this connection that on a recent Chicago radio broadcast the question was posed whether today there were any communities which embodied the ideal set forth in the Acts of the Apostles (cf. Acts 2:44-47). I waited smugly for the answer that religious communities do so, but the answer given was that the Amish communities seemed to be the only signs in our day of genuine Christian community living. Eloquent testimony to the need for religious to measure their lives against their professed ideals!

It is precisely to this exercise that Fr. Murphy-O'Connor beckons us, indeed, forcefully pushes us. His study is all the more valuable because Vatican II, while directing a renewal of religious life, gave less original reflection to this aspect of Church life than to any other. Its value is not limited to providing criteria and guidelines in the process of renewal, however. Most communities have already completed the renewal process (insofar as renewal is ever complete), and the pendulum is beginning to swing back gently to structure. It may swing as it will;

Fr. Murphy-O'Connor's analysis will retain its impact and its validity for it places values and structures, goals and means, in correct relationship.

This balance is achieved by the author's resolve to stay firmly within the bounds of the verifiable and the concrete. Abstractions sometimes serve a necessary purpose, but they do so at the price of drawing out a particular aspect from a larger whole, as the word itself suggests. The insistence in this essay on the real and practical, on the concrete, means in the final analysis that religious life is examined in its entirety. The parts are seen in relation to one another and to the whole. Religious life is viewed as a distinct form of community life within the Church, but not as an entity divorced from the mainstream of Christian life or of humanity.

Those whose responses to the original essay are included in this publication generally recognize its authentic insights, but they also give voice to reservations many will feel on a first reading. In his replies to them the author is given an opportunity to clear up misreadings of his thesis, to adjust the focus of his study more finely, and to develop aspects of it more fully. Some of the responses, such as that of Fr. Francis J. Moloney, make a substantial contribution of their own to the question, "What is religious life?" Others serve to bring out of the shadows dimensions of religious life left there in the long overdue attempt to highlight the apostolic value of living and being together in Christ (as distinct from working together), the aspect which Fr. Murphy-O'Connor rightly insists is specific of religious life. If occasionally the responses and replies verge on acerbity, if occasionally the minds behind the pens seem determined not to meet on the points at issue, more often the exchange is honest, lively, and productive.

As members of religious communities enter upon the task of rewriting their constitutions in the light of their study and experience since Vatican II, they will do well to read or re-read *What Is Religious Life?* Its message, essentially that of the New Testament, must be written ultimately in our hearts, if religious life is to survive and to continue to nourish its members and serve the Church and the world.

Sr. Kathleen Ashe, O. P.
Rosary College
River Forest, Illinois

The 'raison d'être' of religious life

The renewal of religious life is a topic that preoccupies many. A whole series of documents emanating from Rome are devoted to various aspects of the problem. In most countries meetings, seminars, and workshops are held regularly to discuss ways and means of improvement. Younger religious alert to contemporary problems continually argue about 'new forms'. Such concern to infuse new life carries the clear implication that the institution is almost moribund, and this fear is betrayed by the atmosphere of quiet desperation that characterizes many groups. Few novices enter, and fewer remain. A feeling of lassitude permeates the 'in-between' group, those in their 30s and 40s, and they are dismayed at the seeming futility of their lives. To them, very often, religious life contributes nothing that they cannot receive from other sources, and it seems to provide little for the Church beyond a reservoir of cheap labour.

Recognizing this situation many religious ask : why bother? Are we not trying to put new wine into old vessels incapable of containing it? Is all the activity designed to perpetuate an institution that has outlived its usefulness? If not, what is the utility of religious life? Does it have a specific and unique contribution to make?

At first sight it is disconcerting to find how little attention is paid to this fundamental question, but a little reflection makes this silence understandable. Religious communities are performing works of charity whose value is undeniable, and God calls certain individuals to the practice of the 'evangelical counsels' and their value is attested by the New Testament. While capable of explaining the silence, these two reasons do not justify it, because neither is capable of resisting serious examination.

The first reason places the justification for religious life on the level of service. In the concrete the services rendered by religious communities can be classified under two generic headings, teaching and nursing. In so far as these activities are works of charity they are obligatory for all Christians. They are not reserved to a special group who can be said to receive a unique vocation. For many centuries religious had a monopoly on these two types of service within the Catholic Church, but this means nothing more than that religious were more concerned than others to fulfil a fundamental obligation flowing from every Christian's baptism. The situation is a condemnation of those who were not so concerned. It does not point to the specific value of religious life. On the level of practice there is no difference between the mode of operation of a religious school and a lay school, between a religious hospital and a lay hospital. Put the sisters running a hospital into nurses uniforms and no one can tell the difference. To this it will be objected that there is in fact a difference stemming from the dedication of the sisters and brothers. I, however, cannot grant this objection any validity, because fundamentally it is nothing more than an entirely unchristian reflection on the character of vast numbers of totally-committed lay teachers and nurses. The validity of this criticism of one of the traditional justifications for religious life is borne out by the attitude of today's youth who see absolutely no reason to become religious in order to become dedicated teachers and nurses. Any attempt to present religious life to them in terms of this type of service will inevitably fail. Not only is there nothing specifically religious about this type of service, but anyone with average intelligence who feels a call to alleviate ignorance or suffering will reasonably prefer to operate in the context of a well-equipped State institution rather than in a religious institution struggling for money. If one is committed to service, efficiency and effectiveness are valid criteria.

The second reason makes the justification for religious life reside in the authority of Jesus. It is maintained that he offered the grace of following three evangelical counsels to certain privileged souls. He, therefore, founded religious life, and this is a guarantee of its value, even though this value may not be clearly perceived at certain periods of the Church's history. At present we are in the middle of one such period and must struggle on in darkness until the clouds disappear. This view is untenable, because careful study of the New Testament has shown that it contains absolutely no basis for any distinction between two groups of Christians, one group being called to a higher ideal than the other (see, for example,

J. Tillard, 'Le fondement évangélique de la vie religieuse', *Nouvelle Revue Théologique,* 1969, pp. 916-55). In so far as the so-called 'evangelical counsels' exist (and this point will be discussed in some detail in later chapters) they concern *all* Christians. Not only are they offered as the ideal to all Christians but their observance is binding on all in certain circumstances. Religious life is rooted in the New Testament only in so far as it institutionalizes the radicality of these 'counsels'. This may appear to be sufficient justification, but it does not really get to the root of the problem, because many who do not belong to religious communities sincerely strive to live the gospel in all its radicality. It is easy to find examples from our own experience, but in the long history of the Church we can point to the Desert Fathers. They took the gospel message literally and tried to live it, but since they did so in isolation we do not call them 'religious' in the strict sense. What is most distinctive about religious life is not the acceptance of the 'evangelical counsels' as a way of life, but the fact that religious attempt to live this acceptance *in community.* Historically, the distinctive characteristic of a religious is participation in common life.

Hence, the question of the value of religious life turns out to be a question regarding the value of a particular type of community, namely, a community made up of adult individuals of the same sex. It can be taken for granted that there are certain individuals who can survive and be happy only in such a community. To this extent, therefore, it has a value. Normal selection procedures, however, rightly inhibit the acceptance of such individuals. Religious life is not a refuge for the weak, and the best religious are those who could have been a success in any walk of life. A genuine religious community will certainly contribute something to its members, but it contributes nothing that they cannot receive from other sources. This indicates that the value of religious life must be sought in reference to society and the Church. An institution has a function and a value if it meets a need that cannot be satisfied in any other way. Hence, in order to determine whether or not religious life has a value we must look for a need on the part of society and/or the Church which can only be met by this particular type of community.

THE SITUATION OF CONTEMPORARY MAN

According to Aristotle man is a 'social animal'. He needs other human beings in order to live humanly. Heidegger was not saying quite the same thing when he said that 'being-with-others' was a characteristic of human existence, because he was simply describing man's *de facto* situation in which he cannot avoid the company of others. He is thrown into their midst whether he likes it or not. This fact is impressed ever more firmly on our consciousness by the continuing population growth. In fewer and fewer cities can a man afford to possess his own house. He is forced to share a building with others. Society has become so complex that it is virtually impossible for a man to achieve anything entirely on his own. The need for co-operation should be increased by the tremendous progress made in the means of communication. Yet an eminent philosopher can write that 'hell is other people', and a popular song proclaims that 'hell is in "hello" '. More and more people speak of a desire 'to get away from it all' or 'to get out of the rat-race'. This desire indicates an awareness of tension. It betrays the difficulty of living together. But we hardly have to be this subtle. In this century there have been two world wars, but the gaps between them have been filled with numerous little wars. The world has never been completely at peace for over seventy years.

It is hardly surprising, therefore, to sense a note of despair in the question : is it possible for men to live together? Men's hopes have been so often disappointed that they have begun to question seriously the very possibility of any genuine community larger than the family. They speak more frequently of 'co-existence' which is much more an armed truce than a real sharing. Yet this state of affairs is felt to be unnatural. The protest is most evident among the young, and while its volume is certainly traceable to the herd-instinct, it would be foolish to deny that it is rooted in an entirely valid judgement on contemporary society. Many opt out, but the more perceptive do so only as an aspect of their quest for a more human way of living.

Christian theology can only applaude this attitude, because it embodies an insight as old as the more ancient parts of the Old Testament. The unity of the human race is affirmed in the creation narrative (Gen. 1-2) and in the genealogies (Gen. 5 and 10). God intended men to live as brothers in peace and harmony. It was as a result of sin that man could say to God 'Am I my brother's keeper?' (Gen. 4:9), and the division that thereafter split the human race is exemplified by the episode of the tower of Babel which concludes with God's condemnation, 'Let us go down and there confuse their language, that they may not understand one another's speech' (Gen. 11:7). The reality of this judgement is with us to the present. Different languages only symbolize the variety of mental blocks that inhibit mutual understanding, compassion, and tolerance. Because of sin man has ceased to live humanly, and the most urgent of contemporary needs is to recover a truly human mode of existence.

COMMUNITY AND RECONCILIATION

Since sin destroyed not only man's relationship with God but also his relationship with his brethren, Paul was led to see that Christ's ministry of reconciliation embodied both a vertical and a horizontal dimension. The most important text is perhaps Eph. 2:14-16.

He is our peace, who has made us both one, and has broken down the dividing wall of hostility, ... that he might create one new man in place of the two, so making peace [*horizontal dimension*], and might reconcile us both to God in one body through the cross [*vertical dimension*], thereby bringing the hostility to an end.

It is difficult to say whether this text establishes the logical priority of the horizontal dimension over the vertical dimension. In any case, it is not necessary to do so in the present context. What is essential is that the two aspects of Christ's ministry are indissolubly united. There can be no reconciliation with God without reconciliation with one's fellow-men, and no reconciliation with one's fellow men without reconciliation with God. In this passage from Ephesians Paul is speaking formally of the hostility between Jew and Gentile, but that his words have a deeper meaning can be inferred from other passages which are linked to it by the theme of the 'new man'.

You have put on the new man ... where there cannot be Greek and Jew, circumcized and uncircumcized, barbarian, Scythian, slave, freeman, but Christ is all in all (Col. 3:10).
As many of you as were baptized into Christ have put on Christ. There is neither Jew nor Greek, neither slave nor freeman, neither male nor female, because you are all one man in Christ Jesus (Gal. 3:27-28).

The saving-event who is Christ signals the end of the condemnation of Babel. Through Christ mankind is once again offered the pristine harmony in which God created it. Man is presented with the opportunity of emerging from the egocentric isolation in which he has immured himself.

It is because he is isolated that man is subject to the pressure of sin (cf. Rom. 3:9; 5:12; 5:21; 6:6, 23). Sin in this sense is a mythical figure created by Paul to symbolize the corroding force of a corrupt environment. Imperceptibly and inevitably man absorbs the orientation of his sin-influenced environment, and eventually intensifies its force by contributing his own attitudes. Since no one can escape the influence of his environment man-without-Christ is enslaved to sin. He may recognize his condition, and regret the wall of hostility he almost unwillingly raises against his neighbours, but he can do nothing about it. Man-in-Christ, however, is 'no longer enslaved to sin' (Rom. 6:6). 'No longer' are the operative words here. Christ's victory over sin was not a complete suppression. Sin is still active. Christ's victory was a redemption through which man was removed from the power of sin. If sin is in fact the all-pervasive pollution of a corrupt environment, man can only be removed from the power of sin by being transferred to a different environment. An example will make my meaning clear. Take the case of a poor asthmatic living in a highly-industrialized area. The atmosphere that he cannot avoid breathing is impregnated with fumes that are highly detrimental to his condition. No doctor can save him simply by *telling* him to go and live where the air is pure. He has to give him the means to get out of the atmosphere that will be his death. He has to show him where clear air is to be found, and to transfer him there, for only there can the asthmatic find the breath of life. Paul characterized the law as impotent to save man because it did no more than tell him to alter his way of life. Christ, however, created a new environment in which man could truly live, and this new environment is nothing other than the Christian community.

Only in this community does man enjoy 'freedom'. He is freed from hostile pressures that inhibit his development. He is freed to become himself, that self that God willed from the beginning. Only in the Christian community does man come 'alive' (Col. 2:13 and *passim*). As we have seen, the more perceptive characterize contemporary existence as 'non-human', and this insight harmonizes perfectly with Paul's view that existence without Christ was 'death'.

No one speaks of a corpse as 'human'. It is respected only for what it *was*. Those who exist under the power of sin are not truly living. Their mode of being does not display the humanity that God intended. For Paul, to live as men, to enjoy specifically human existence, is possible only in the Christian community. If this view seems strange and artificial we should question our understanding of 'humanity'. Whence do we draw our idea of 'humanity'? Is it based on men as we see them all around us? If so, we should stop and take stock. In a truly Christian perspective man is defined by the extent to which he actualizes his capacity for love. Can we honestly say that contemporary man does this to any appreciable extent? He lives in a world characterized by broken marriages and broken treaties, by bitterness and anguish, by suspicion and dread, by war and starvation – and he is far from satisfied with himself.

The Church, therefore, has the answer to the world's need. It offers to the world true community where 'love binds everything together in perfect harmony' (Col. 3:14) and in which man can again begin to live humanly. What one has and what the other lacks correspond so perfectly that the failure to communicate is a major problem. It has long been recognized as such, but the reasons for the failure have been insufficiently analyzed.

AUTHENTIC PROCLAMATION

This type of failure to communicate can have two possible culprits, the Church or the world. Too many casually assume that the latter is the culprit : hte world *refuses* to listen. I find this answer impossible to accept, because the world's need is too great and too widely shared. Furthermore, it is surely more Christian to begin with self-examination.

One reason why the Church's proclamation is not accepted is because it is not on the same plane as the world's question. This question is asked on the level of living, but it is answered on the level of words. The world is *told* that true community is possible, but it asks to be *shown*. It must be recognized that promises have little or no credibility today. The world has been deceived too often. The only convincing argument in favour of a theory today is that it in fact works, that it not only promises but delivers. The Christian answer to the problem of community will appeal to the world only when it is seen to work in practice. Only an existential affirmation is acceptable, as Paul recognized when he wrote to the Philippians :

> Do all things without grumbling or questioning, that you may be blameless and sincere, children of God without blemish in the midst of a crooked and perverse generation, among whom you shine as lights in the world, holding forth the word of life (Phil. 2:14-16).

Genuine community carries with it a new form of 'life', by comparison with which the ordinary existence of mankind can only be characterized as 'death'. A word capable of bringing men who are 'dead' (in specifically human terms) to 'life' is preached only by living, because only life can generate life. The Christian community of Philippi did not engage in what we would term 'apostolic activity'. It did not preach in the sense of pronouncing words. Nevertheless the very quality of its existence was a proclamation, and only such proclamation can be called 'the word of life', a term that Paul never applies to his own verbal preaching. Not only is this type of existential affirmation the only one that is genuinely adapted to contemporary needs, but it is the only one that is truly Christian. In the new dispensation God's invitation to man is not a spoken word as it was in the old dispensation but a person. His word was incarnated in Jesus Christ. Authentic Christian preaching must preserve that incarnational mode. Words must take second place to the fundamental affirmation that is the quality of Christian life.

THE RAISON D'ETRE OF RELIGIOUS LIFE

At this point in my argumentation it might seem that I have thought myself into a corner, because what has been said is applicable to *the Church*. I have shown that Paul considered a genuine Christian community as the only possible form of proclamation that says anything to men divided by hostility, and it must be admitted that the community of which Paul was speaking is the Church. He never said anything about religious life in the technical sense in which we use that term.

The first point to be made in response to this objection is a theological one. Within the Church religious are not a caste apart as are bishops, priests, and deacons. They belong to the laity and have no special place in the hierarchical structure of the Church. They are not called to a higher ideal than the ordinary Christian, nor are they called to a more perfect observance of the same ideal. Hence, what is said in the New Testament of Christian life in general can be applied strictly and literally to religious life.

The second point to be made in response to the objection is that when Paul speaks of the Church he does not mean the universal Church, he means a local Church. The Church of God is an abstract concept which only becomes real in a local community. Thus, for example, Paul writes 'The Church of God which *is* in Corinth' (1 Cor. 1:2; 2 Cor. 1:1). Even if this is admitted, we must go further and specify that Paul's 'local Church' bears no resemblance to the contemporary diocese or parish. The point is not the institutionalization of the contemporary diocese or parish, but its *size*. The average parish in Western Europe or the Americas is much bigger than any of the Pauline communities, and paradoxically, size in this case makes for invisibility. The average diocese cannot be *seen* to be a community, because its membership is geographically dispersed. Proportionally, the same is true of any parish so numerous that the members cannot be accommodated at a single liturgical celebration. The diocese and the parish theoretically are communities. One might infer, therefore, that they have a witness value. Theoretically one could agree, but realistically one must dissent, because witness is a matter of life not of theory. Visibility is of the essence of existential witness, since it is a non-verbal affirmation. Today only two communities are capable of furnishing the existential witness that Paul attributes to the local Church, the family and the religious community.

The justification for religious life lies in the fact that its witness potential is much greater than that of the family. We must be extremely realistic when talking about witness. For too long we have been satisfied that truth is proclaimed. It is a step forward to recognize that the proclamation must be by the quality of life and not simply by word of mouth, but the state of the world demands that we examine the effectiveness of existential affirmation. Two criteria can be applied; capacity to catch the attention of the negligent, and capacity to minimize the loop-holes through which the mind escapes to avoid confrontation. Judged by these criteria the witness value of the family is inferior to that of the religious community. In the first place, the family is a natural unit. No one, therefore, is surprised to encounter it; its very existence has no shock value. The religious community, on the other hand, forces itself on the attention of the world, precisely because it is unnatural by the world's standards. Witness the morbid curiosity that surrounds religious communities in non-Catholic areas. In the second place, a happily unified family can be explained in natural terms. Its evident happiness may in fact spring from a deep Christian faith which has been the prime factor in surmounting difficulties, but it is too easy to avoid seeing this relationship, because it can be explained in terms of sex or the attraction of blood. The same loop-holes do not exist when the community is composed of adults of the same sex, as is the case with the religious community. Of course, it can always be said that the existence of the community is due to homosexual attraction, but slight acquaintance with even a single member of the community is sufficient to dispel this objection designed to explain away the community.

It goes without saying that in the concrete many families give greater witness than religious communities, and that a group of individuals of the same sex living in the same building do not automatically give witness. Witness, as we have seen, is a matter of the quality of life, and this point will be discussed in more detail in subsequent chapters. Here, I am content to make the point that the witness *potential* of the religious community is superior to that of the family, because this is sufficient to justify the existence of religious community. Both the gospel and the world demand an existential affirmation of the possibility of true community, and in *practice* the religious community is the only one capable of giving this witness. Such witness could be given by the Christian family, but because it is a natural unit it is too easily discounted to be really effective. The diocese and the parish are in theory capable of giving this witness, but given the complexity of contemporary life it is impossible to see how this theory could be reduced to practice. However, should this ever happen on a sufficiently wide scale, then religious life will have no *raison d'être*. As things stand at present, religious life is the one force calling the parish and the diocese to true community. It is a sign of hope not only to the world but also to the Church. In terms of altruistic love, of mutual sharing of goods, and of submission to the call of God in Christ the religious community is what the diocese and the parish are called to be. The religious differs from the layman or woman only in so far as the religious has formally assumed the responsibility of manifesting in community the horizontal dimension of the ministry of Christ.

It is not without significance that religious communities began to be formed at precisely the moment that Christianity became the official religion of the empire. Prior to that time the local community, or Church, was small and cohesive, because its environment was hostile. There were no social advantages to being a Christian, and many disadvantages. Members knew each other and were dependent on each other for survival, because their ranks were periodically thinned by persecutions. As a result, the community-Church was visible both to its members, and to those outside who cared to look. With the establishment of Christianity, membership in the despised sect was seen to have definite advantages, and whole cities and countries became Christian. The Church became a social institution, and bureaucracy and ceremony conspired to push the element of true community into the background. It was then that certain individuals began to see the difference between the Church as they knew it and the first Christian communities, and to recreate deliberately the ideal described in the Acts of the Apostles :

> All those who believed were together and had all things in common, and they sold their possessions and goods and distributed them to all, as any had need. And day by day, attending the Temple together, and breaking bread in their houses, they partook of food with glad and generous hearts, singing God's praises, and having favour with all the people. And day by day the Lord added to their number those who were being saved (Acts 2:44-47).

Thus the original religious communities were simply modelled on the first diocese, as John Cassian (fourth century) recognized when he wrote that the first religious went apart 'to practice those things which they had learned to have been ordered by the apostles throughout the body of the Church in general' (Conf. 18, c. 5).

The founders of the first communities had the profound insight that in such communities the Christian was 'freer' to seek perfection. Whether consciously or not this was an attempt to recapture the realism of Paul's concept, an attempt to make it mean something on a concrete practical level. An ambience was created in which the pursuit of the Christian ideal would not be hindered by inimical pressures. From the beginning, therefore, the religious community had a value for the individual who entered it. Unfortu-

nately, this aspect received a distorted emphasis at the beginning
of the religious movement, because the sentence immediately preceding the above quotation from John Cassian runs : 'Those who
still maintained the fervour of the apostles, mindful of that former
perfection, left their cities and intercourse with those who thought
that carelessness and a laxer life was permissible to themselves
and to the Church of God, and began to live in rural and more
sequestered places.' We find here a note of disdainful withdrawal
which is in radical disagreement with Luke's portrait of the Jerusalem community. This latter group was essentially outward-looking,
eager that all should share the new values that shaped the existence of its members. The impact of its existential witness is
evident in the note that it 'had favour with all the people'.

Despite the distortion noted above, the first communities preserved the fundamental insight that the religious community is for
the individual. Paradoxically, as religious communities gradually
returned to the outward-looking attitude of the original Jerusalem
community of Acts, this aspect was pushed into the background.
Religious communities acquired a social function by providing
services (e.g. education), and as these services became social neces-
sities the religious was gradually made subordinate to the service-
apostolate of the community. The needs of the individual did not
weigh against the needs of the apostolate. The apostolate came to
be regarded as the common good of the community to which the
individual was obliged to make a contribution. In the next chapter
we shall see that this attitude has had disastrous consequences for
the understanding of authority in religious communities, not to
mention many individual lives. The fact that the services traditionally provided by religious communities are being taken over more
efficiently by other organizations is an undisguised blessing. It has
produced much heart-searching and despair, but it has also served
to focus our attention on the authentic function of a Christian
community according to the New Testament, and has thus revealed
the perennial value of religious life.

It goes without saying that members of religious communities
will continue to render service. I am not advocating that they
should sit down and simply *be*. What is important is that religious
recognize that the primary service they render to the Church and
to the world is the witness of their life together as a community.
Only in this way is adequate witness given to the horizontal dimension of Christ's mission. Only in this way is the world's agonized

question answered. Once the primacy of the existential witness provided by the quality of community life is firmly established, the community can undertake, either corporately or individually, any of the works of mercy. Material services have their place, but this is very definitely a secondary one. Because human nature is what it is, there will be a continual temptation to reverse the priorities, and to transfer the emphasis from the primary (existential witness) to the secondary element (material services). There is an intangibility about existential witness that leaves us unsatisfied. Since we find encouragement in success and stimulus in failure we feel a need to measure the effectiveness of our apostolate. Thus we are unconsciously and imperceptibly pressured to give the primacy to services whose effects are capable of measurement. However, we must die to ourselves, we must be prepared to make the sacrifice involved in renunciation of certain knowledge. Anything else is an evasion of our responsibility, and the destruction of our *raison d'être* as religious.

Authority and community

Authority and community are co-relatives, not only in the sense that one is never found without the other, but also in the sense that a particular community demands a particular type of authority. There are specifically different types of community and each one enjoys its appropriate form of authority. The functions legitimately assumed by authority in one type of community can be diametrically opposed to the true nature of another type of community, and when the two are mismated we have the real source of all problems concerning authority. Hence, it will be necessary to analyze in some detail the three specifically distinct forms of community, and to determine the form of authority approrpiate to each. While the religious community fits neatly into *one* category of community, it will be seen that the understanding of authority commonly found in religious communities owes something to all

three categories. Little wonder that we have a crisis of authority!
It will become evident, however, that in many cases the so-called
'crisis' is nothing less than a praiseworthy rejection of an inappro-
priate form of authority.

THE ACTION-COMMUNITY

The action-community is a community whose *raison d'être* is the
performance of a series of related actions. An army, for example,
exists in order to execute a plan of defence or attack; a business
company exists in order to produce and sell a product; the appar-
atus of State exists to perform functions beyond the capacity of the
individual. The role of authority in such a community is to initiate
and co-ordinate the actions appropriate to the end of the community. Without this guiding force the end would become impossible.

According to the *Shorter Oxford Dictionary* authority is defined
as : 'The power or right to enforce obedience; the right to command or give an ultimate decision.' This definition is accurate *only*
within the context of an action-community; it is entirely inadequate with respect to the two other types of community. The role
of authority in an army is to formulate a plan of attack or defence,
and to see that it is executed. From this function is derived the
right to command individuals to play their part in the over-all
plan, and to reward or punish them as the need arises.

In an action-community the individual takes second place to the
plan which represents the common-good of that community. However, the individual is not totally subject to the common good,
because this particular common-good is limited by the nature of
the community. The authority vested in army officers demands a
certain totality in the response of the soldier, but since the object
of that authority is exclusively action, the totality that authority
can command is limited to the level of activity. The soldier's
internal attitudes are entirely outside the competence of military
authority. As long as he does what he is told the legitimate
demands of authority are satisfied. The fundamental evil of the
totalitarian State is precisely what is implied in its name. It
demands total response in *all* areas of human life, whereas its
authority is limited to the sphere of action. It has the legitimate
right to impose taxes, but it has no right to attempt to control
what citizens think about taxes.

These principles are very simple in their theoretical statement, but on the practical level complications very quickly appear. Thought, for example, has a definite influence on the quality of action. Someone who judges an action useless or positively harmful will not perform as well as one who fully approves. In many instances the quality of the action is irrelevant, but this is not always true. It is of no importance whether one pays one's taxes enthusiastically or not, but failure to co-operate fully in attack or defence can mean needless loss of life. In such cases authority cannot resort to the type of thought-control that is implied in brainwashing, but it is within its rights in taking into account, not only intelligence and physical ability, but also mental attitude, in its selection of personnel. Authority in an action-community commands respect if the plan is apt to the goal to be achieved, and if individuals are assigned to roles that they have the capacity to fulfil.

Even though a religious congregation is not an action-community, the understanding of the function of authority that is appropriate to this type of community is very often clearly perceptible in the exercise of religious authority. This is an inevitable consequence of the prevalent tendency to justify religious life in terms of service. To put the primary emphasis on the services rendered by the community is to impose on it the characteristics of an action-community. If the community thinks of itself as dedicated to getting things done, it is inevitable that authority in the community will consider itself responsible for ensuring that things do in fact get done. Individuals will be assigned because there are slots to be filled, and they will be assigned to positions for which they have neither the taste nor the ability, because there is no one else and the job has to be done. Authority will naturally attempt to assign round pegs to round holes, but in the last analysis it does not really matter if the peg is in fact square. The suffering that this causes is brushed off as one of the purifying factors of religious life. In this situation one finds as little genuine dialogue between the religious and his/her superior as between an army officer and his subordinate. This parallel is not at all far-fetched, because the constitutions of very many religious congregations have been deeply influenced by the concept of the 'Church militant' which is one of the most pernicious ideas ever introduced into Christian theology. The Church does in fact fight against evil, but to infer from this that the Church has the characteristics of an army is an utter perversion, because it has diverted the Church's energy into channels that have proved totally unproductive. Ever since the idea was introduced the world has become progressively less Christian.

The most unfortunate consequence of the tendency to consider the religious community as an action-community is the fact that the quality of life and action is pushed entirely into the background. Authority concerns itself exclusively with the accomplishment of the action, and in practice cares nothing for its quality. More importance is given to punctuality and efficiency than to the quality of Christian love which should inform the action. A teacher who is a religious is judged on his or her ability to get students through exams, never on his or her ability to communicate Christian values in such a way that they truly become part of the student's personality. Such authority rarely, if ever, attempts to motivate a religious. It concerns itself with this aspect of its function by providing an annual retreat and monthly lectures.

It is precisely those superiors who conceive their authority as 'the power or right to enforce obedience; the right to command or give an ultimate decision' who cry most loudly about a crisis of authority. The reaction of younger religious against this understanding of authority could be interpreted as instinctive reaction against the view that a religious community is an action-community. However, it is an unfortunate paradox that it is these sam⌐ younger religious who are most concerned about service. They see more clearly than their elders the social needs of their environment, and very often the point of their 'rebellion' is to be freer to give themselves to non-traditional forms of service. They are often more explicitly ocncerned than their elders to infuse their actions with genuine love, but unless they give absolute primacy to quality, they will continue to draw upon themselves the type of authority proper to an action-community, and they will nullify the only basis on which they can legitimately object to this type of authority.

THE COMMUNITY OF THE PERFECT

Opposed to the action-community is the community of being. This is a community whose members gather together not in order to do something, as in the action-community, but in order to be or become something. The easiest example of a community of being is a fitness club whose members join together in order to become fit and healthy, or in order to remain in condition. The distinction between 'being' and 'becoming' points to two sub-categories within the community of being, which can be termed the community of the perfect and the formation community.

The understanding of the Christian community as a community of the perfect has surfaced periodically throughout the history of the Church. The principal support for this concept is to be found in certain statements scattered throughout the Johannine literature, e.g. 'No one born of God commits sin, for God's nature abides in him and he cannot sin because he is born of God' (1 John 3:9). However, the Church has always condemned this understanding, because it is based on a highly-selective reading of the New Testament. In the same epistle from which the above quotation is drawn we also read : 'If we say we have no sin, we deceive ourselves, and the truth is not in us' (2:8). Nevertheless, it is a curious fact that certain characteristics of the type of authority proper to a community of the perfect are to be found in the exercise of authority within the Church.

What I have in mind has been finely suggested by Rosemary Haughton in her study of one of the historical manifestations of the community of the perfect.

> The doctrinal and ritual quarrels, the splits and feuds, the back-biting and accusations of heresy, are almost too involved to be unwound, and all of them show the basic assumption that correctness of doctrine and behaviour are the essential proof, to oneself and others, of being saved. 'Deviationism' and moral failings of any kind, were proof not of being *unconverted* but of having *fallen* from one's conversion, and being therefore, in a state of reprobation. This was such a terrible thought, especially in connection with one's own children, that any amount of harsh discipline and punishment was used in order to terrify the young and wayward into that outward conformity that would prove their right to be regarded as members of the Church. . . . Hypocrisy is inevitable under such a system, and smugness and talebearing equally so. Also the fears and passions which might not be openly expressed or indulged could be legitimately worked off by hounding those whose behaviour branded them as the devil's children (*The Transformation of Man,* London, 1967, pp. 205-6).

It would be easy to parallel this account with aspects of the techniques employed by the Inquisition and its successor the Holy

Office, and one is very tempted to do so because it involves the paradox that the official guardians of the faith operated under an assumption based on a condemned doctrine. However, my concern here is with the manifestations of this attitude in the exercise of authority in religious life.

It seems undeniable that the understanding of religious life as 'a state of perfection' has had a definite influence. What precisely 'state of perfection' means is difficult to determine, because it is certain that no religious thought of himself as perfect. It seems likely, however, that the constitutions and customs of any religious congregation were considered to exhibit the pattern of behaviour appropriate to a community of saints. This can be inferred from the fact that fidelity of observance is the prime criterion for the canonization of a religious. By their vows, and in particular by the vow of obedience, religious were considered to have committed themselves to a pattern of behaviour appropriate to perfection. In other words, they were supposed to act *as if* they were perfect. That they in fact were not was passed over in silence, in the pious hope that by acting as the perfect act they would eventually become perfect. The dishonesty of this approach is too obvious to need emphasis.

Given the assumption that the rule of the community proposes a pattern of behaviour appropriate to sanctity, it is inevitable that authority should be paternalistic. It conceives its function as being protective and preventative. The most efficient way to protect the individual from himself and to prevent mistakes is to take away all initiative and to minimize the possibilities for personal judgement. This is done by filling the day with minutely detailed duties, and by making it obligatory to request permission for any situation not covered by rule or established custom.

Given the original assumption this attitude on the part of authority is entirely logical. The validity of the original assumption is called into question by lack of any foundation either in the New Testament or in the history of the Church, but its falsehood is made manifest by the consequences of this understanding of authority. It results in a complete distortion of the priorities of the gospel. Faith, hope, and charity are the ingredients of sanctity, but they are impossible to legislate for. In practice, therefore, they take second place to the observance of the rule. From the point of view of authority to miss a community function is much more serious than to miss an opportunity to show love. Charity was tolerated only within the framework of the rule. Thus, for example, it could not be true charity to speak to a fellow-religious in deep personal trouble once the bell had rung for solemn silence. It is never presumed that any deviation from the rule might be motivated by a valid reason; one immediately becomes suspect of self-indulgence. Since self-indulgence is the antithesis of sanctity, the 'devout' feel themselves empowered to sniff around for deviations, and placate authority by insisting that something be done about it. To bring someone back to the narrow path of righteousness is true charity. Yet how can there be true charity without trust? The atmosphere of suspicion is carried to the point where personal friendships are considered dangerous. And how can there be true community without friendship? The active concern, trust, and growth that are the characteristics of friendship are the social manifestation of charity. In other words, the existential witness that is the justification for religious life is made impossible by this understanding of authority, because it identifies uniformity with genuine unity of mind and heart. It is assumed that community exists, but the impression given to outsiders has been well put by Rosemary Haughton : 'It was like trying to behave *as if* you lived in a house, with doors and stairs, when you are really camping in a field. The result looks lunatic to the outside observer, though it seems perfectly consistent to the deluded, as they mount their imaginary stairs and meticulously lock non-existent doors' (*op. cit.*, p. 209).

THE FORMATION COMMUNITY

In the first article we saw that the religious community is a microcosm of the Church. It manifests to the world the values that the Church is intended to manifest, and it serves to stimulate and inspire the Church to realize these values. It follows, therefore, that the religious community is the same type of community as the Church. This is important because in the New Testament it appears clearly that the Church is not an action-community, but a community of being, and that within this second category it is not a community of the perfect but a community of those in the process of formation. Many passages could be cited in support of this assertion, but one will have to suffice here.

Not that I have already obtained this or am already perfect. But I press on to make it my own, because Christ Jesus has made me his own. Brethren, I do not consider that I have made it my own, but one thing I do, forgetting what lies behind and straining forward to what lies ahead, I press on towards the goal for the prize of the upward call in Christ Jesus. Let those of us who are mature be thus minded, and if in anything you are otherwise minded, God will reveal that also to you (Phil. 3:12-15).

The last sentence of this text hints at divergent views in the Pauline communities, but Paul's good-humoured tolerance, and his confidence that the truth will win out in the end is an object lesson in some of the qualities of true leadership. There is no ambiguity about his view that the Christian community is not an association of the saved, but a privileged opportunity to work towards salvation.

THE CHARACTERISTICS OF A FORMATION COMMUNITY

The formation community is first and foremost a community of opportunity. It is a setting which aids something to happen to the member. Since the formation community with which we are concerned is the Church, and by implication religious community, this 'something' is the deepening of faith, hope, and love, the intensification of identification with Jesus Christ. In other words, the community provides the conditions which enable man to become what God originally destined him to be, that is, fully and consciously human. This, it should be remembered, is the fundamental lesson of the incarnation. God *became man* in Jesus Christ. As followers of Christ we in turn must become men. True humanity is not something given. In man there is no inexorably programmed evolution to maturity as in the case of the animals. What makes Christianity unique among world religions is the fact that it has given man a concrete model for his inarticulate, sometimes unconscious, aspirations. Jesus is the invitation of the Father, but he is also the perfect fulfilment of God's design for his human creation. In his humanity he is the living demonstration of the consequences of acceptance of the divine invitation.

Recognition of Christ as the divine offer of friendship is the only condition for membership in the Christian community. This recognition is a grace, and it is a conversion. This conversion is never complete in itself, but implies the commitment to work towards its deepening, that is, towards the complete transformation of the entire personality in the line of the original conversion, to the point where the individual becomes progressively more capable of mirroring to mankind the response who was Christ.

The first requirement in order that such continuing conversion be a real possibility is freedom from pressure hostile to the original commitment to Christ. In other words, the believer must be protected from the power of sin. Concretely this freedom is guaranteed by the sincerity of the commitment of all the other members of the community. Since 'bad company ruins good morals' (1 Cor. 15:33), the fundamental service they render each other is the elementary one of good example. This mutual support is the bulwark of Christian freedom.

Mutual support implies a positive element that goes beyond the negative element of freedom from pressure. The positive thrust emanating from the members of the community is, in the ultimate analysis, the attraction of the ideal towards which the community aspires. Historically, no movement has retained the high level of mutual support necessary for survival, unless this ideal is incarnated in a symbolic centre exercising a centripetal force that draws the individual members into true community. To be the symbolic centre is the function of authority in a formation community.

AUTHORITY IN A FORMATION COMMUNITY

As we have seen the formation community is a sub-division of the community of being. To illustrate the community of being I proposed the example of a fitness club. It will be advantageous to analyze this example in some detail. The utility of the example is increased by the frequent use made by Paul of sportive images in order to illustrate the Christian life (cf. 1 Cor. 9:24; 2 Cor. 4:7-9; Gal. 5:7; Phil. 3:12-14; 1 Tim. 4:7).

The function of the authority-figure in a fitness club is to show the members how to become and remain fit. In addition he must inspire them to effectively desire this goal. Of course, this desire is already present in those who become members, but the role of authority is to intensify this desire, and to sustain it in the face of other pressures. In order to fulfil this role it is evident that the authority-figure must possess something more than knowledge of the demands and limits of the human body, and of the techniques of exercise. He must embody the fitness that others seek to achieve. The beneficial results of glowing health must be so evident in him that others are stimulated to emulate his achievement.

This type of club has some obvious points of similarity to the action-community. Its training rules correspond to State legislation and military commands. This is one of the reasons why the two types of community are frequently confused. However, if we look a little more closely it becomes evident that the rules have an entirely different value in an action-community and in a community of being. In an action-community commands are absolutely essential and must be obeyed. Without them the community could not achieve its goal. In a community of being, on the other hand, rules are useful but not essential. The members of the fitness club can achieve their goal by imitating the techniques of the fittest member who is the authority-figure. In his person he releases the power of the ideal to which the members are attuned.

Since the goal of the members of a fitness club is that each one interiorize the ideal of optimum health, it follows that the club has no common-good distinct from the achievement of the individual member. This points to a second major difference between the action-community and the community of being. In the former the individual is for the community in the sense that the individual is used in order to realize the goal of the community. The individual, of course, benefits from the prosperity and security of the state, but built into the structure of the action-community is the assumption that a number of individuals are going to be losers. They can forfeit their lives in the army, and taxes can wipe them out economically. When religious life is treated as an action-community individuals are assigned to positions that do not exploit their talents and which stunt their growth. From the point of view of authority this is unfortunate, but it is a small price to pay for the common good. A community of being, on the contrary, is for the individual in the sense that the *raison d'être* of the community is the success of the individual. Thus for one member to fail means that the whole community has failed.

Such failure is to be traced ultimately to lack of adequate motivation, and this brings us to the third difference between an action-community and a community of being. Authority in an action-community only needs to know. The general must know how to plan effectively, but it is not necessary that he have the physical capacity to execute the order he gives. A tax-collector has to know how to return accurate accounts, but it is not necessary that he be an honest man in the fullest sense. Knowledge alone is not sufficient in a community of being. A sickly individual could only inspire contempt in a fitness club, even if he had an expert's knowledge of the techniques of exercise. While his advice may be acceptable, he cannot be said to exercise real leadership. Such leadership depends on personal qualities other than intelligence, which permit him to motivate members because of what he *is*. Authority in a community of being must be able to inspire a genuine willingness to struggle through to success which is possession of the ideal. On the contrary, in an action-community authority cannot motivate positively, it can only threaten. No soldier acts bravely precisely because he wants to win a medal, and no one pays taxes in order to be considered a model citizen, but both can be forced to act because of fear of the consequences. A soldier may be inspired by love of his country but that motivation is not supplied by military authority.

With these considerations based on the nature of a community of being in mind we can now turn to the New Testament, and we find that our attention is drawn to aspects that have not received due attention in discussions of Christian authority.

The religious community as a microcosm of the Church is a faith-community which exists in response to a divine call expressed in a person, Christ. The goal of the members is to follow Christ as perfectly as possible. Hence, their most fundamental need is to know Christ, not just in an abstract historical way, but as a person whose appeal they feel. The challenge of faith becomes real and vital only when the divine demand is rearticulated in a personal form, that is, in a personality who can say with utter conviction 'for me to live is Christ' (Phil. 1:21).

This fundamental need was recognized by Paul. He repeated the traditional Judaeo-Hellenistic theme that men should aspire to live like God, but he went a step further. To the Ephesians he wrote : 'Be imitators of God, as beloved children, and walk in love, as Christ loved us and gave himself up for us, a fragrant offering and sacrifice to God' (5:1-2). The community is exhorted to imitate the Father as well-loved children always do. But imitation demands direct experience. Hence, Paul presents Christ as the concrete model. To imitate God Christians have only to love as Christ loved, that is, completely, utterly, to the bitter end. But here we have the same difficulty, only on a different level. How many Christians have direct experience of Christ? Paul could write as he did, because he had personally encountered Christ, and the result of this experience was that he could say, 'It is no longer I who live, but Christ who lives in me' (Gal. 2:2). The communities for which he was responsible had never met Christ. They had never seen him in action or experienced the power of his personality. Yet Christ was the focal point of their conversion, and must be the centre around which their lives evolved and developed. Since Paul was aware of the deep human need for a concrete demonstration of the real possibility of a preached doctrine, he took the only possible step and proclaimed, 'Become imitators of me, as I am an imitator of Christ' (1 Cor. 11:1).

This extraordinary statement is not unique. Something similar is found in all the letters addressed to communities that knew Paul personally (cf. 1Thess. 1:6; 1 Cor. 4:16-17; Gal. 4:12; Phil. 4:9). It would have been unrealistic to have addressed the same admonition to the Romans, Colossians, or Ephesians, communities that had never known Paul in the flesh! It cannot be dismissed as an insignificant 'aside', but must be considered an essential element in the apostle's understanding of his own authority. Moreover, this idea is not peculiar to Paul. Peter wrote to the local leaders of his community, 'Tend the flock of God that is in your charge, not by constraint but willingly, not for shameful gain but eagerly, not as domineering over those in your charge, but being examples to the flock' (1 Peter. 5:2-3). The notion that leaders might have to be forced to serve underlines his awareness of the tremendous responsibility it carries (cf. also 1 Tim. 3:1). This responsibility is not discharged by 'domineering' (literally, 'acting as lord'), because this is the type of authority appropriate only to an action-community, but by living lives worthy of imitation. 'I have given you an example, that you also should do as I have done to you' (John 13:15). Hence, the importance of the leader's motivation ('Willingly', 'eagerly'), because this alone gives an intrinsic transcendental quality to actions. Paul's awareness of the importance of his presence as a stimulus to the believer's following of Christ is well brought out in that passage of Philippians where he argues the advantages of death and life (1:21-26). On entirely personal grounds he would prefer to die because that would mean closer union with Christ, but his sense of apostolic responsibility outweighs this selfish desire, and he concludes, 'To remain in the flesh is more necessary on your account. Convinced of this, I know that I shall remain and continue with you all, for your progress and joy in the faith.'

A little reflection shows that it could not be otherwise in a Christian community. A Christian community is founded on the incar-

nation, an act which introduced a new mode into God's relationship with mankind. No longer can that relationship simply be
spoken about, for this mode is proper to the old dispensation which
has been superseded. It must be reincarnated. It is only in this
perspective that a traditional statement such as 'the voice of
authority is the voice of God' can be given a *specifically Christian*
interpretation. In the Old Testament God spoke, but in the New
Testament he conceived and uttered a Word, the person of Christ.
The word that the bearer of Christian authority 'speaks' is his own
personality as transformed by Christ. Unless he is 'another Christ'
no one has genuine authority in a Christian community.

To the extent that he reincarnates Christ, the authority-figure
also incarnates the ideal towards which all the members of the
community strive. He thus exercises a centripetal force which draws
them together to constitute the whole Christ. As the reincarnation
of Christ, the authority-figure is the head which is a source of
vitality for all the members (cf. Col. 2:19). Such authority is
encouragement and inspiration because it shows that the ideal is a
real possibility and not merely a matter of theoretical speculation.

Only such authority can demand the 'complete obedience' that
has traditionally been exacted from religious. Paul's concept of
'obedience' is here very instructive. He never speaks of obedience to
the will of God, and he never refers to the response to a law or a
precept as obedience. Obedience is given only to Christ (2 Cor.
10:5-6) or to the gospel (Rom. 10:16; Gal. 2:14; 5:7), and these
two are in reality but one and the same, since the gospel is nothing
more than the prolongation of the mission of Christ, which is
carried forward not only by Paul's words but by his person. Hence,
Paul can speak of 'the obedience of faith' (Rom. 1:5), that is, the
obedience which is faith, and 'faith' in the Pauline sense is the
total commitment of the believer to Christ. The ideal proposed to
humanity in Christ necessarily involves this totality because it is
nothing less than the full development of human life in God's
plan. Christian authority has the right to total response only insofar
as it incarnates this ideal which is the response that Christ gave to
the Father. Thus the demands of authority in a community of
being are legitimately much more radical than in an action-community where it can only command the partial response of the personality since its competence is limited to the level of action.

Only this understanding of 'obedience' leaves entirely intact the
individual's initiative and responsibility. He is under authority

insofar as it reincarnates Christ. The quality of leadership which is
'the upward call in Christ Jesus' (Phil. 3:14) continually summons
him to give himself more completely. However, the concrete modality of his response is left to his own decision. It could hardly be
otherwise in a formation community because maturity is acquired
only through the exercise of responsibility. The community exists in
order to inspire authentic decisions, but it cannot make mistakes
impossible.

It is easy to foresee the objections to which this concept of
'obedience' will give rise. Were it accepted a religious might, for
example, decline to accept an assignment. However, a specific task
has importance only within the context of an assumption that we
have seen to be false, namely, that a religious community is an
action-community. The witness value of religious life consists in the
quality of its corporate existence, not in the furnishing of specific
services, and the quality of corporate witness depends on the quality
of each member's life. Unless the members are seen to be maturely
responsible the community as a whole can have no witness value.
Thus, in the ultimate analysis, the witness value of the community
depends on it being a setting in which members can make decisions
regarding their own lives. Objections will also stem from the fear of
chaos in religious communities. One must conceed that this fear is
justified, but only because in the common understanding of authority and obedience members are permitted no real responsibility.
As a result they remain immature, and are inevitably irresponsible
in their use of freedom when it is given them. They naturally
react like children who have been kept too long under strict
discipline. It is not to be wondered at that the majority of religious
communities today have little or no witness value, and that today's
youth finds nothing attractive in religious life. It is not true that
religious life is not meant to be 'attractive'. Idealistic youth find
challenge attractive, not comfort and ease. And when they
encounter a concept of authority and obedience which is in opposition to the New Testament, they discover only stagnation.

On the contrary, to understand obedience as the context of
freedom imposes a much greater burden of responsibility on the
individual, because he is continually faced with the obligation of
choice. No longer can he hide behind a directive of authority, but
he must work out for himself what God demands of him in any
given situation, and as Paul well knew this is a matter of 'fear and
trembling' (Phil. 2 :12). Authority does no service to the community

if it attempts to take away this the sole opportunity for genuinely human growth.

Similarly, the type of Christian authority described in the New Testament makes many more demands on the superior. No longer is it sufficient to know the rule and constitutions, to be an administrator, to have the capacity for making decisions. There is the fundamental obligation, in Paul's terminology, of 'being changed from glory to glory' (2 Cor. 3:18). In both Old and New Testaments 'glory' connotes a visible, effective manifestation of God, and Paul simply means that the image of Christ in the believer should become progressively more manifest. This obligation rests on all Christians, but it weighs particularly heavily on religious whose *raison d'être* is the witness value of their lives. A fortiori, therefore, it binds the superior whose prime function it is to inspire the transformation into Christ of the members of his community. Christian authority is a function of sanctity, but this should not frighten us. As part of a formation community the superior is himself in the process of transformation. What is essential is that the superior be a relatively more perfect embodiment of the ideal than the other members of the community, because otherwise he cannot communicate the inspiration and encouragement that is their basic need.

Even such a superior will find it necessary to act authoritatively. While Paul strongly affirmed the incarnational mode as the fundamental form of community building, he also found it necessary to give a great many specific directives. I have discussed the significance of these directives elsewhere,[1] and I mention the point here because silence might be misunderstood. It also gives me the opportunity to emphasize that rules and constitutions of religious congregations and the directives of superiors have precisely the same utilitarian value. Any impression that authority is deciding for the religious must be scrupulously avoided. The role of authority is to present material for a decision that the maturing member of the community will take for himself. A truly mature decision demands that *all* aspects of the concrete situation be taken into account. Through lack of experience or carelessness an individual may ignore one or more aspects. If so, authority is genuinely formative in bringing them to his attention. Within the context of the radical, non-verbal, Christ-like inspiration that is essential to the very exis-

1. 'The Contemporary Value of Pauline Moral Imperatives', *Doctrine and Life* (February 1971), pp. 59-71.

tence of the community, such assistance will be entirely acceptable. To do this correctly, however, demands great insight on the part of the superior. He must know when to press for a decision, and when a decision would be premature. He must know when a religious is capable of responding authentically, and when he is likely to be frightened into evasion, that is, purely external conformism. The exercise of authority on the conscious level is, therefore, an agonizing process, because the superior will never have sufficient certitude before the fact to be sure that he is acting correctly. However, if the effort is inspired by genuine love, no error will be irreparable, particularly if the conscious effort is sustained by Christ-like quality of life.

The so-called contemporary crisis of authority is a myth. The disarray cannot be traced to contempt for authority. It has finally been recognized that authority that operates by means of decree alone is not Christian. Meek submission to paternalistic discipline has been replaced by a desire for real leadership. Naturally this worries those in authority, because when they were appointed their sanctity was not the dominant criterion. If they have any integrity they cannot recover their peace of mind by a return to the old ways, because that would be a contravention of the gospel. However, in fairness to them it must be pointed out that superiors can be destroyed by their communities. A superior who genuinely tries to lead may be swamped by bureaucratic requests, by being drawn into disputes within the community which should be settled by those immediately involved, by being forced to make decisions for those who will not assume their inalienable responsibility. We live in a time of opportunity and light, not in a time of crisis, and the responsibility for a return to gospel values of authority and obedience rests equally on all.

To sum up : The *raison d'être* of a religious community consists in the witness value of its corporate existence. This can be only if the lives of individual members of the community command respect and admiration on the part of outsiders. They must, therefore, be fully mature Christians. The community exists to give them this opportunity. It can do so only if the ideal which calls them, namely Christ, is reincarnated in the person of the leader who is the symbolic centre without which true community is impossible. Simply by *being* he reveals the others to themselves, and inspires and enourages their efforts towards ever more complete configuration to Christ.

Prayer of petition
and community

When we speak of community prayer we think normally of the Mass and the Office. The Office is an occasion where the whole community joins together to praise and thank God for the call to salvation which brought it into being. At Mass the community participates in the sacrifice of the cross, the sacrament of the faith and love that it must witness to the world. As Rosemary Haughton has so convincingly shown, the Mass is also a community prayer in a much more profound sense.[1] It is a ritually staged encounter with the sacred, which parallels the conversion narratives in the gospels, and which is designed to challenge, and thereby deepen, the faith of the participants. Taken seriously it is not simply a prayer *of* the community, but a prayer which *builds* the faith-community. When properly understood the prayer of petition produces the same effect.

THE INFALLIBILITY OF PRAYER

The most striking feature of the New Testament teaching on the prayer of petition is its emphasis on the infallibility of such prayer. One has only to put forward a request and it will certainly be answered. The promise is absolute and, with the self-evident exception of faith, no conditions are laid down. The briefest form of this promise reads, 'Whatever you ask in prayer, you will receive, if you have faith' (Mt. 21:22; Mark 11:33). A more extensive and graphic form appears in the Sermon on the Mount :

> Ask and it will be given to you. Seek and you will find. Knock and it will be opened to you. For everyone who asks receives, and he who seeks finds, and to him who knocks it will be opened. What man of you, if his son asks him for bread will give him a stone? Or if he asks for fish will give him a serpent? If you then who are evil know how to give good gifts to your children, how much more will your Father who is in heaven give good things to those who ask him (Mt. 7:7-11).

1. *The Act of Love* (London 1968).

This passage presents no exegetical difficulties. The words can bear only their obvious and natural meaning, and the underlying imagery is based on the social structure of a semitic society where even an adult son is dependent on his father for the means of sustenance. A slightly different version of this saying is found in Luke 11:9-13, and it is generally agreed that the Lukan form is a later adaptation of the form found in Matthew. Only one point of difference need concern us here, because it points to the key difficulty of this passage, namely, that we make petitions which are not answered, despite the absolute character of the promise of Jesus. In place of Matthew's 'How much more will your Father who is in heaven give *good things* to those who ask him', Luke has, 'How much more will your Father who is in heaven give *a holy spirit* to those who ask him'. The meaning of 'good things' is very wide, and is capable of covering both material and spiritual realities. 'A holy spirit', on the other hand, is severely limited to spiritual realities. This can only be an attempt to minimize the factual contradiction between promise and fulfilment. Petitions for material realities were in fact not fulfilled, and so Luke limited the promise to the sphere of spiritual realities which are intangible, thus taking the promise out of the realm where verification is possible.

The theologians have found various explanations for God's silence in the face of man's requests. What we asked for was not really good for us. We did not ask with sufficient faith. Our prayer was answered, but in a fashion that we did not recognize. To anyone who has ever begged God in real need, these 'explanations' have a very hollow ring. When the poor ask for bread it is undeniably good that they should get it, and according to the New Testament when they ask for food they are promised food, not a substitute. To say that they are accorded the grace of patience is to make a travesty of theology. It is equally unreal to say that they must lack faith if their petition is not answered, because in many cases this inference must cede before the counter-indications in individual lives of great personal faith. These cannot be ignored or swept aside in order to enable theologians to construct facile theories.

THE GOD TO WHOM WE PRAY

Fundamental to all such theories is the assumption that if petitions are not answered it must be due to a fault on the part of the petitioner. At first sight this assumption appears entirely reasonable, because God is all-powerful and can do exactly what he wishes. If God does not respond, it must be because he does not wish to do so, and since God is a loving Father, this must be because the petitioner has given him cause. At this point, however, we run into an impasse, as we have seen above. The fact that the so-called 'explanations' are untenable should cause us to question the validity of the underlying assumption. But is any other assumption possible? If it is denied that the reason for non-response lies with the petitioner, we are forced to say that it lies with God. Since it would be absurd to suggest that the reason is to be found in God as he is in himself, because he is loving omnipotence, we are constrained to examine more closely God as he is in his mode of acting.

The problem can be situated very precisely by means of the question : to what God do we pray? It is a facile oversimplification to say that the question is meaningless because there is only one God. Jews do not view the one God in the same way as do Christians, because for the Jews God did not become incarnate whereas for the Christians he did. Thus when Christians pray, they pray not to the distant God of the Old Testament, but to the Father who took flesh in Jesus Christ. As a result the prayers found in the New Testament are addressed indiscriminately to the Father and to Christ (e.g. Rom. 1:7; 1 Cor. 1:3, etc.). This focusing attention on Christ opens the way to a further question : where is Christ? To say that he is with the Father is only a half truth. A different perspective is provided by another passage of the first gospel which speaks of the infallibility of prayer :

> I say to you, if two of you agree on earth about anything they ask, it will be done for them by my Father in heaven. For where two or three are gathered in my name, there am I in the midst of them (Mt. 18:19-20).

The God who answers prayer is the God who is in Christ who is *in the community*. This mysterious identification of Christ with the Christian community is a major theme in Matthew because the whole gospel is bracketed by the two affirmations, 'Behold, a virgin shall conceive and bear a son, and his name shall be called Emmanuel, which means "God *with us*" ' (1:23), and 'All authority in heaven and on earth has been given to me. Go, therefore, and

make disciples of all nations ... teaching them to observe all that
I have commanded you; and behold, *I am with you always,* to the
close of the age' (28:18-20). Precisely the same idea is ennun-
ciated in Christ's question to Paul on the Damascus road, 'Saul,
Saul, why do you persecute *me?*' (Acts 9:4), because Christ says
'me' rather than 'mine', even though Paul was in fact persecuting
the Christian community. The theme also appears in the Johannine
literature, for example, 'If a man loves me, he will keep my word,
and my Father will love him, and we will come to him and *make
our home with him*' (John 14:23).

It is this 'God-with-us' who answers prayers. At this point we
must ask the question that theologians consistently ignore, 'How?'
The answer is suggested by the saying that Matthew juxtaposes to
the saying on the infallibility of prayer :

> If you then who are evil, know how to give good gifts to your
> children, how much more will your Father who is in heaven
> give good things to those who ask him. *So whatever you wish
> that men would do to you, do so to them* (Mt. 7:11-12).

The italicized sentence, known as the golden rule, is found in a
different context in Luke's version of the Sermon (6:31). The
majority opinion among exegetes is that Matthew transferred it
from that position to its present one in his gospel. This view has
been called into question recently, principally because no good
reason was proposed to motivate the transfer. My suggestion reme-
dies this deficiency, because I believe that Matthew faced the problem posed by the saying on the infallibility of prayer, as did Luke,
but came to a different solution. The link between the two sayings
is provided by the necessary association between 'desiring' and
'asking'. One only asks for that which one desires. This directs our
attention to the response. In the first saying we have 'your Father
who is in heaven', and in the second 'men will do'. The intimate
union between 'desiring' and 'asking' suggests that a similar union
is to be found here. This can only be, however, if men are
inspired by the same love that motivates the Father, and this is
precisely what is indicated, because the golden rule is a rule of
reciprocity. Its observance supposes a union of love in which the
needs of one automatically become an obligation for o thers.
Matthew who is *par excellence* the theologian of community saw
that petitions are infallibly answered if the petitioner lives in a

community of love. The existence of a community of love is the
Father's fundamental gift, as we have seen previously, because the
efforts of sinful man alone cannot bring it about. In answering
prayers God preserves the incarnational mode inaugurated by the
sending of his Son.

The same idea appears, though less clearly, in the Johannine
writings where Jesus is presented as saying :

> If you abide in me, and my words abide in you, ask whatever
> you will, and it shall be done for you (John 15:7).

The careful chiastic arrangement of John 15:7-17 indicates that
vv. 16-17 provide the key to the interpretation of this statement :

> You did not choose me, but I chose you and appointed you
> that you should go and bear fruit and that your fruit should
> abide; so that whatever you ask the Father in my name, he
> may give it to you. This I command you, to love one another.

What is 'abiding in Christ' in the concrete but to belong in a fully
committed way to the Christian community? What are the 'words'
that must abide in us, but the precept of mutual love in its various
forms? What is 'bearing fruit' but love in action? Putting all these
elements together it becomes clear that the Father's response is
mediated through a loving community. Where love reigns, it is
sufficient to express a need for it to be met. This conclusion is
confirmed by a passage from the first epistle of John :

> Beloved, if God so loved us, we also ought to love one another.
> No man has ever seen God. If we love one another God abides
> in us and his love is perfected in us (4:11-12).

The Christian community is the 'perfection' of God's love in that
it is the prolongation of the love which God expressed in Christ and
is the contemporary active expression of that love. Since 'God is
love' (1 John 4:16), the reality of God is made manifest in the
mutual exchange of love which constitutes true Christian community. God is not present in a group no matter how orthodox doctri-
nally but which merely speaks of love, and if he is not present how
can he respond to those who ask? 'If anyone has the world's goods
and sees his brother in need, yet closes his heart against him, how

does God's love abide in him? Little children, let us not love in word or speech but in deed and in truth' (1 John 3:17-18).

The conclusion is clear. If prayers are not answered it is we who are responsible. If prayers are answered it is we who answer them. This is not to say that the only way in which God can act is through the Christian community. Miracles can happen, and there are no limits on God's mode of acting. However, if we recognize the authority of the New Testament, we must admit that the normal mode of God's response is the incarnational one.

RESPONSIBILITY AND PRAYER

If at first sight this conclusion appears shocking, a little reflection on the consequences of the one alternative, namely, that God normally works in mysterious (i.e. non-human) ways, should give pause for thought. Take, for example, a case that is unfortunately far from rare. A young religious decided to leave religious life. For a whole year before she had agonized over her decision. Her distress had been obvious, yet no one had approached with an offer of help. Shortly after she had left she got a letter from an older sister who was manifestly concerned at her departure, and who, among other things, wrote : 'Several times last year I noticed that you were very unsettled, and I prayed for you very fervently. Now I feel that God has rejected my prayers.' The older sister was worried, and anxious to help, but she was not sure that she would fully understand and doubted her ability to cope. God, on the other hand, was all-wise and all-powerful. Hence, she relieved her mind by entrusting the matter to his hands. Was her attitude truly Christian?

An affirmative answer is impossible. What she did was to *substitute* prayer for action. She saw a human need and she shrank from responding personally. She contented herself with passing the responsibility to someone else. Her motives for so doing are irrelevant because 'love bears all things, believes all things, hopes all things, endures all things' (1 Cor. 13:7). In the last analysis, her prayers were not answered because she did not love enough. Genuine love takes no heed of possible rebuffs. Genuine love knows that while it may not be able to solve problems it can communicate hope and encouragement, it can engender the tranquillity in which the materials for decision become clearer. These were the objects of the older sister's prayer, and it was she who failed, not God. To blame God was a further evasion of responsibility.

Such irresponsibility is inevitable, given an understanding of the prayer of petition which permits the substitution of prayer for active concern. Hence, the importance of emphasizing that the normal mode of God's response is through the Christian community. To pray is a grace, but the grace is not in the words, but in the insight into the need which prompts the petition. For a Christian, to recognize a need is to assume responsibility for meeting it. Otherwise how can the love that is supposed to be the characteristic of Christians be a reality? If I personally lack the resources to meet a need, my responsibility obliges me to seek out one who has the required capacity. Only when all possible avenues have been explored is it permissible to entrust the matter to God alone, and to absolve oneself from further effort.

Another consequence of the assumption that God does not normally work through incarnational channels is irreality in prayer. It is pointless to pray for the enlightenment or the encouragement of the major superior of a religious congregation and to leave it at that. The means to enlightenment is rational argumentation presented in a convincing way. The means to encouragement is to tell him or her that he or she is providing the leadership that the congregation needs. God is not going to work a miracle when he has provided these normal channels of grace. Similarly, it is unrealistic to pray vaguely for world peace. World peace can only come about if there are many islands of peace which progressively enlarge themselves to the point where they all link up. Through Christ God has given mankind the key to peace, and the responsibility to make peace is ours. To imagine that God needs to have the problem pointed out to him is infantile. A certain school of theologians has fantisized that God will intervene directly provided that a divinely ordained condition is fulfilled, namely, that a certain number of petitions are made to God. The point of prayer of petition, therefore, is to meet this condition. If God does not act, it can only be because sufficient prayers have not been said. Such a travesty could only have been concocted by theologians dedicated to word-games, never by Christians committed to loving. God was aware of the problem before we were, and he has already provided the solution, the lesson of the life of Christ. Peace is potentially there, and we do not fulfil our responsibility to make it a reality by simply talking about it, even to God. If we pray, our prayer must be that of St Francis, 'Let me be an instrument of thy peace.' We must be prepared to spend the time and effort to get to know the facts of divisive situations. We must be prepared to devote all our understanding and ingenuity to discovering ways of bringing opposing parties together. We must be prepared to suffer rebuffs and set-backs without number. Nothing less is Christian.

Since authentic Christian prayer necessarily involves the expenditure of energy, it follows that our prayer becomes progressively less authentic as its object is more remote from our concrete environment. The reason is very simple. Our resources, both psychic and physical, are limited, and the more we spend abroad the less we have to spend at home. To concentrate on influencing distant situations means that we are less effective in our local situation, and that is where our prime responsibility lies. It is laudable to be actively interested in the poor of India, only if that does not distract us from the plight of the poor in the next street. There are many who will back up their prayer for the poor of India with material contributions, but who will not give *of themselves* to the poor next door. Yet this is what the gospel demands. Were all Christians as concerned in deed as they are in word for the needs of their immediate environment there would be energy to spare for the needs of those more distant. But until that is achieved the good must not be permitted to become the enemy of the better. The inadequacy of its sense of reality is one of the major causes of Christianity's lack of real witness value.

ASKING AND RECEIVING

The implications of this understanding of the prayer of petition for community are clear but need to be emphasized. If I am convinced that I, under God, am responsible for answering the prayers of my brethren, and if they recognize that they are responsible for answering my prayers, there is no room for the type of evasion that is destructive of community life, and a force is let loose which generates community.

To pray for others means that a need has been expressed or recognized. On the surface a need that has been explicitly articulated poses no problem. Take, for example, the request, 'pray for my brother'. For a Christian it is not sufficient to mention the matter to God. The request is an appeal for help, and while addressed to God it is also addressed to a specific human individual. Two people are involved, the petitioner and his brother. To discover the root of the trouble may involve some subtlety, but to help these two people as they need to be helped demands more than good-will. Great sensitivity is needed, because each individual is different, and their real needs may only be hinted at in the words they use. The same type of sensitivity comes into play when the other cannot articulate his need, either because of inhibitions or because he does not know himself well enough.

This sensitivity is called 'discernment' by St Paul. The Greek term he uses is drawn from medical language, and in its original sense is denoted the ability of a born doctor to make a correct diagnosis without sufficient empirical evidence. To be blessed with 'discernment' was to be the possessor of a highly refined intuitive judgement. The value of such a judgement in community life hardly needs comment. Were all possessed of it the misunderstandings that cause tension would disappear. Hence, Paul prayed 'that your love may abound more and more, with knowledge and all discernment, so that you may approve the things that really matter' (Phil. 1:9-10). Contrary to the scholastics who maintained that love was consequent on knowledge, Paul here underlines that it is love that gives the capacity to truly know. Insight is directly proportioned to love. The more one loves the greater one's insight into the needs of the beloved. Thus, from another point of view, we see that the effectiveness of our prayer is conditioned by our capacity to love.

Love grows only through mutual exchange in a community of love, and this is what the Christian community is meant to be. What is love in the concrete but trust, confidence, and concern? If I really believe that the God who listens and answers is the God who is incarnate in my brethren, I will open myself to them in a way that leaves no barriers. I will trust myself to them on the deepest levels of my personality. I will confidently admit my need for them. Possessed by the same belief they will act likewise. This is what community is all about, and such an attitude towards the prayer of petition is the literal expression of community. It expresses what it is, and builds it towards what it can be. In it will be found the intense reciprocity of active love which is the essence of the witness value which is the *raison d'être* of Christian community.

A community discussion that is honest, trusting and personal is perhaps the closest contemporary approximation to this ideal. The adjectives 'honest, trusting, and personal' are important, because I am not concerned with the type of community meeting which contents itself with the discussion of practical details, such as, the horarium or the amount of pocket-money. I have in mind a group in which each member speaks honestly of his or her expectations of community, in which each trusts the others with the expression of his or her needs as an individual in community, in which true charity is shows by the common striving towards a consensus regarding the meaning of their lives together. In such a meeting many petitions are made, and they are answered by the community. However, there is a very definite value in going a step further and addressing these petitions formally to God in Christ, because it is a necessary reminder of what the Christian community is. It exists due to the benevolence of the Father, and it needs continually to express that relationship.

This highlights the importance of the prayer of the faithful. In many places it has degenerated into a sterile formula in which intercession is made, without any commitment, for Pope and bishops – but it can be revitalized very easily. Authority in the community can use it to bring to the attention of the members collective needs. Individuals can use it to bring into focus their own needs and those of others. In effect, all that has to be done is to make the petitions' more personal and more realistic, and to remember that when we say in response, 'Lord, hear us' we address ourselves as other Christs and the community as the whole Christ. By so bringing to consciousness our awareness of our responsibility for the community and our dependence on it, we open ourselves to the challenge to our faith which is presented in the Mass. Only by loving can we begin to comprehend the sacrifice of love. Only by truly loving in Christ do we share the bread that is love.

Poverty and community

Long before the establishment of religious communities a life of poverty attracted many as an expression of the Christian ideal. It was inevitable that this radical understanding of the demand of Christ should have influenced those who founded the first communities, and ever since poverty has remained one of the structural characteristics of religious life. Nonetheless it must be recognized that few aspects of religious life give rise to more problems on the practical level. Guilt feelings are engendered by the fact that reli-

gious communities are not 'poor'. They maintain a standard of
living superior to that of the turly underprivileged in their society.
As a result, religious who have to listen to the old joke 'you take
the vow of poverty and we keep it' begin to feel that their vow is
a meaningless formality, an assertion which by its insincerity
destroys the witness-value of religious life. This tension has been
resolved in different ways. Some abandon all reference to religious
poverty and proclaim the intention of 'living like the rest of the
world', while others make a consistent effort to strip themselves of
worldly goods in order to attain the state of insecurity that characterizes the truly poor. Judged in the light of the New Testament
both these solutions are wrong. The former fails to recognize the
inner dynamic that gives community life its witness value. The
latter rests on a radical misunderstanding of the gospel message.

SHARED EXISTENCE

For Paul man is a Christian if he exists 'in Christ'. This phrase has
given rise to endless discussions among scholars, because the pre-
position 'in' can have several meanings in Greek. However, grammar
alone cannot provide the answer. Only the assimilation of Paul's
whole Christology can reveal the density of meaning that he packs
into this lapidary phrase. Because of the limitations of space a
complete exposition is not possible here, but we can take a short-cut
by looking at two intimately related Pauline statements. The Christian is a 'new man', and he exists as such by 'putting on Christ'.
Through their use in sermons these terms have been banalized into
synonyms for self-improvement. Paul, however, uses them in quite
a different sense. In his theology they have a collective, not an
individual, value. The two principal texts are :

> You have *put on the new man* ... *where* there cannot be
> Greek and Jew, circumcized and uncircumcized, barbarian,
> Scythian, slave, freeman, but Christ is all in all (Col. 3:10).
>   As many of you as were baptized into Christ have *put on
> Christ*. There is neither Jew nor Greek, neither slave nor free-
> man, neither male nor female, because *you are all one man in
> Christ Jesus* (Gal. 3:27-28).

The similarity of these texts is obvious. They share the 'putting on'
metaphor, and the lists of traditionally hostile groups. Both make

the point that 'in the new man' and 'in Christ' such divisions no longer exist. According to Galatians all constitute 'one man' in Christ, and to this 'new man' Collosians applies the very significant particle *'where'*, which indicates that the 'new man' is a spacial concept. The 'new man' that each believer is exhorted to put on is not a new set of moral habits, but a sphere of existence of which others are also part. In other words, our existence as Christians is not something that we personally possess. It is something in which we participate or share. It would have been impossible for Paul to conceive of an autonomous Christian. It is only in the union of other Christians that man is 'alive in Christ'.

If the Pauline letters are read in this perspective many familiar texts are seen to contain a more profound depth of meaning. Paul's statement to the Romans that 'None of us lives to himself, and none of us dies to himself' (14:7) is very frequently taken to mean that no Christian should be selfish. But this is not what the text says. It is a purely factual statement regarding the nature of Christian existence. No genuine Christian can live for himself, because his very existence is not his own. It is something that he enjoys in dependence on others. He *is* as a Christian in and through them. This is the reason why selfishness is the antithesis of Christianity. Paul insists on unselfishness so frequently because it is the essential element in the inner dynamic of Christian existence. To *be* for others is the only mode of existence that is Christian, since the Christian *is* only because of others equally committed to Christ. In this perspective it is natural that the generosity of love should be the law of the Christian. It is the one form of activity that is the adequate expression of his very being. This insight is crucial for any adequate understanding of both religious poverty and religious celibacy.

POVERTY AND COMMUNITY

The insight that the Christian and his community are mutually dependent was recognized explicitly in the Jerusalem community of whose life we get glimpses in the Acts of the Apostles :

> And all who believed were together and had all things in common, and they sold their possessions and goods and distributed them to all, as any had need (2:44-45).

Now the company of those who believed were of one heart and soul, and no one said that any of the things which he possessed was his own, but they had everything in common. ... There was not a needy person among them, for as many as were possessors of lands or houses sold them, and brought the proceeds of what was sold, and laid it at the feet of the apostles, and distribution was made to each as any had need (4:32-35).

Two points emerge with great clarity from these texts. The first Christians did not divest themselves of their wealth as if this were a good in itself. They did so in order to raise the standard of living of needy members of the same community. The emphasis is on giving to others, and stripping oneself is only a means to this end. All possessions were held in common in order that no one might be in want. The handing over of material goods was a symbol of the sustaining love which constitutes the reality of Christian community. This apparently is the meaning of the curious episode of Ananias and his wife Sapphira (Acts 5 :1-11). Peter makes it clear that they had no obligation to surrender their wealth. They sinned by pretending to donate all, when in fact they were contributing only a part. Their lie was the facade of total dedication which cloaked a radical selfishness.

By handing over their wealth in order to ensure the subsistence of others, the first Christians caused them to 'live' on a very concrete physical level. Equally, by stripping themselves of their proper means of subsistence they made themselves dependent on the community for their physical life. Thus they brought to the level of tangible expression the mutual interdependence on the level of being that we have seen to be the essence of Christian life. Common life witnessed to the world the reality of the community of being.

Christian poverty, therefore, has two facets, complete personal depossession *and* the capacity to make a contribution to the material well-being of the other members of the community. There is a paradox here which makes it worth while to look at each of these aspects in some detail.

PERSONAL DEPOSSESSION

For the New Testament complete personal depossession, i.e. the lack of the means of subsistence, is not a good. Real indigence is in contradiction with the very nature of the kingdom of God. It is generally recognized that the form of the Beatitudes in Luke is more primitive than that in Matthew, and reflects more exactly an eschatological proclamation to the underprivileged :

> Blessed are you poor, for yours is the kingdom of God.
> Blessed are you that hunger now, for you shall be satisfied.
> Blessed are you that weep now, for you shall laugh (6 :20-21).

The idea that the Messiah would put an end to economic deprivation is very clear in the Old Testament, and is taken up by Jesus in the synagogue at Nazareth when he proclaims the fulfilment of the prophecy of Isaiah :

> He has sent me to proclaim release to the captives
> and recovering of sight to the blind,
> to set at liberty those who are oppressed (Luke 4:18).

The poor are 'blessed', not because of their poverty, but because they have the infallible promise of release from its chains. The day of salvation has arrived and they can rejoice in anticipation of their deliverance. It is presumed that the underprivileged will welcome the proclamation of the kingdom because they have no reason to be content with the *status quo.* Discontent is a necessary prerequisite for faith, because without it there is no openness to a new future. This is what Matthew rather awkwardly tries to convey by his addition to the first Beatitude : 'Blessed are the *poor in spirit,* for theirs is the kingdom of heaven' (5 :3). Taken literally 'poverty of spirit' is a vice, as is indicated by our condemnatory use of the phrase 'he has no spirit'. Matthew is not referring to 'spiritual poverty', but to the spiritual attitude that in many cases accompanies the insecurity of indigence. It is this openness that is significant from a religious point of view, and it must be emphasized that it is not necessarily related to indigence. 'Those who weep now' in the third Beatitude of Luke are also considered to be open in the same way, and the rich also weep. In itself possession of wealth is no obstacle to the kingdom of God, but in many cases it in fact is.

It is important to keep this in mind when reading those texts which associate the renunciation of material goods with the following of Jesus. The most important passage is the episode of the Rich Young Man (Mark 10:17-22 and parallels; cf. R. Haughton, *The*

Act of Love, London, 1968, pp. 34-39). It is clear from the way the evangelists present him that the young man is idealistic. He inherited wealth with a high ethical standard in its administration. He felt a real responsibility for those dependent on him. Yet he was not satisfied. He felt instinctively that there must be something more, and that Jesus held the key. Jesus, we are told, loved him, but he told him, 'Go sell everything you own, and give the money to the poor, and you will have treasure in heaven; then, come follow me.' The radicality of this demand has drawn many courageous hearts, but it has also blocked the obvious question. It must be asked *why* Jesus imposed this condition in this case, because he did not demand the same of other disciples. The fishermen abandoned work (Mark 1:16-20), and the tax-collector left his post (Mark 2:14), but there is no hint that the former sold their boats and nets, or that the latter got rid of his savings. The clue is in the young man's question, 'What must *I do* to inherit eternal life?' Jesus' condition regarding his wealth was designed to shock him out of his complacent desire to retain the initiative, and to indicate the unconditional commitment, without control, without security, without possibility of return, that is the one way to 'treasure in heaven'. The young man looked for a secure bridge from the present to the future. Jesus, in reply, showed him the void of faith, and told him to jump in taking with him nothing but trust and hope.

The episode of the Rich Young Man, therefore, is essentially a narrative revealing the true nature of faith. It only incidentally concerns poverty. The demand to renounce wealth occupies the same structural place as the demand to renounce family ties and obligations (cf. Mt. 8:18-22). Wealth and affective relations *can* be an obstacle to commitment, but this does not mean that *only* the underprivileged and the celibate can attain sanctity.

The point made in the story of the Rich Young Man concerns all Christians. It is not directed to an elite class, because the exigencies of faith are the same for all. The believer must be free of wealth in the sense that possessions must not limit his perspectives, but he is obliged to put them aside only if and when they constitute an obstacle to faith.

The vow of poverty is the act of faith that the Rich Young Man refused to make, and it resonates throughout the whole life of the religious. Not only is his state a continuous gesture of confidence in the future, but by the fact of having placed himself in financial dependence on the community he has acquired a concrete stimulus to reflection on his dependence on the community on the level of his very being as a Christian. In terms of material goods he cannot be sufficient to himself. Since he has nothing he cannot live to himself or from himself. This mirrors the more profound reality of the spiritual plane where he exists only as a member of the whole Christ which, in the perspective of Paul, has reality solely in the local community.

CONTRIBUTION TO THE NEEDS OF OTHERS

Since this dependence is in community, it can obviously be no more than one facet of the reality. The community could not survive unless it is balanced by the assumption of active responsibility for others. If the existence of the Christian in community is a sharing, then all must be productive. Each must generate the faith, hope and love that sustains others. Similar productivity is demanded on the level of material goods. But if the religious has donated all his possessions, how can he contribute to the community on this level? Only one answer is possible, by remunerative work. One of the characteristics of being underprivileged is that one *has* to work in order to live. In the New Testament what distinguishes the 'rich' from other social classes is the fact that they are not bound to labour; they can make capital work for them.

The idea that the ideal of poverty is to have nothing, and to wait for God to send bread from heaven, is attractive to many because it seems to be complete acceptance of the radicalism of the gospel. This, it is maintained, is real dependence on God, and anything else is an affront to divine providence. In reality this view is nothing more than crass theological materialism, and it has played only a very minor and totally aberrant role in the history of religious life. From the very beginning it was considered that religious communities should work to meet their own needs. Pachomios, the founder of the cenobitic life, hired out himself and his monks during the harvest season. Basil the Great demanded that all his monks have a trade. Francis of Assisi, the poet of poverty, took pride in the fact that he earned his own living, and ordered his brethren to continue the trade they had when they entered, and he permitted them to beg only when there was no work, or when the salary was not enough to live on (*Regula Prima*, 7; *Test.*, 19-22). The healthy common-sense that is the antidote to

sentimental forms of radicalism is finely expressed by Cyril of
Scythopolis in his *Life of Saint Euthymius.*

> Since those who live in the world accept the strain and fatigue
> of their work in order to nourish wife and children, to offer to
> God the first fruits, to do good insofar as they are able, and in
> addition find themselves subject to taxes, it would indeed be
> strange that we, rather than being the lazy and immobile
> beneficiaries of the labour of others, should not by means of
> manual labour supply our own material needs, particularly
> when the apostle commanded that the lazy have no right to eat.

The work of a religious community is a point of insertion into the
wider community which is the *raison d'être* of its existence. It *is*
in order to provide a focal point and stimulus for the transformation of the Christian community as a whole. It is not meant to be a
burden. Respect is an essential ingredient of witness, and those who
have to work in order to live respect only those who work equally
hard. The worker-priests who assumed the burden of long hours on
the assembly-line found a hearing denied to those who pontificated
from comfortable parochial houses. For the vast majority of workers
the only real satisfaction is in their salary, because their work in
itself contributes but a very small part to the finished product of
their organization. This engenders a feeling of frustration which
adds to the burden of work. Because of the vow of poverty the work
of a religious is subject to the same frustration but in a slightly
different way. He may be fortunate enough to have a type of work
which permits him to see clearly his contribution to the finished
product, but because the salary is contributed to the community, his
frustration comes in the way in which the fruits of his labour are
dispensed. It may be wasted, or spent on projects with which he is
in disagreement. Such frustration, however, has a very definite
value in the perspective of witness, because Paul underlines that
only those who share can witness. 'Become as I am, *because I
become as you*' (Gal. 4:12). Similarly, Christ could say 'follow me'
only because he had become like us.

POVERTY AND WITNESS

We have seen that the *raison d'être* of the religious community lies
in its capacity to mirror in a concrete and tangible way what the

Christian community should be. It is nothing more than a micro-cosm of the Christian community as such. Its value is a witness value, and such witness is given by truly *being* a community, each member contributing to and living from the love that is its exis-tence. The vow of poverty intensifies the witness value of the community because it is one means of giving tangible expression to the circle of love in which the member both gives and takes. With regard to wealth the religious is under no greater obligation than any other Christian. Detachment is not a perfection to which he alone has access. He does in fact assume a greater detachment, because by the vow of poverty he accepts the responsibility of giving and taking *everything* from the community. The difference between the religious and the ordinary Christian lay-man, there-fore, is only one of degree. But this difference is necessary if the religious community is to fulfil the witness-function that is its *raison d'être*. It is more radical than the wider Christian com-munity, because otherwise it would not stand out sufficiently to be remarked.

What is of supreme importance, therefore, is that the *action* of giving and taking be seen as an expression of the *being* that is given and taken. Apart from that the vow of poverty has no value. It is often said that the vow of poverty frees the religious from financial worries and that, in consequence, its value resides in the greater possibilities for service that it offers. Not only does this interpretation reflect an understanding of religious life with which I cannot agree, but it is an interpretation which does not apply to all religious. Today, particularly, superiors and bursars have more financial worries than any husband or wife. To claim that they are freed by their vow of poverty supposes a concept of freedom that is totally at variance with the reality. It is precisely the type of double-talk that completely destroys the credibility of religious life in the eyes of young people. By their standards of honesty one cannot be free from financial worries when one has in fact to worry about money. This difficulty disappears, if the vow of poverty is presented as a heightened sense of responsibility for the material well-being of the community. This responsibility devolves on all members, since it is but a facet of their love for all. If it is focused more sharply in the cases of superiors and bursars, this is only because they have accepted this service to the community. The vow of poverty must be kept within the context of community in order to have any witness value. Individuals outside community have taken and lived this vow, but their gesture has witness-value only on the level of their generosity to a community. In religious communities the vow has witness-value only if the complex of relationships that unite the members of the community is such as to provoke admiration and respect on the part of those outside.

It is impossible to be more specific. Paul tries to get across the same idea by using the Greek term *kalos*. The lives of Christians both individually and collectively are intended to have this quality: 'We are God's children created in Christ Jesus for *kala erga*' (Eph. 2:10). The normal translation of the final two words is 'good works', but this fails completely to render the resonance of the original. To a Greek *kalos* connotes dignity, nobility, sensitivity, beauty, loveliness, graciousness, proportion, balance, perfection, serenity, in short all that provokes respect and admiration. It is not a type of action, but a quality that can inform any action. It is that, for example, which distinguishes a great painting or piece of music from a mediocre one. The difference is visible, even though it is impossible to pin down in intellectual categories. The reciprocal dependence and productivity that is the essence of the vow of poverty does not have this quality of itself. It acquires it only if it is motivated by love of an exceptional quality.

It is much easier to draw attention to factors that obscure the relationship between the vow of poverty and the life of the community. The residence of a community in a big institution such as a school or college is such a factor. The disadvantage here is not so much the appearance of great wealth, because all reasonable people realize the resources a college or school must have if it is to fulfil its function adequately. However, the personal element tends to get lost behind the institutional aspect. Individual members of the community are seen as parts of a whole, but that whole tends to be the college or school, rather than the religious community, with the result that they are seen as functionaries rather than as religious. The greater visibility of the college or school means that for all practical purposes the religious community becomes invisible. In theory, of course, the two are completely distinct, and everyone knows that religious teachers wear two hats, one as a teacher and one as a religious. It must be emphasized, however, that what is true in theory is irrelevant as far as witness is concerned, because witness exists on the level of what can be *seen* with average good-will. It is not a question here of any difference between theory and practice. The lives of those who live in a community attached to a

big institution are much more difficult and involve many more
sacrifices than the lives of those in small communities. The point
is that such lives are much less visible, and without visibility there
is no witness. For this reason it would be much better were the
community residence completely separated from the institutional
plant.

Today, fortunately, there is a strong tendency towards small
communities, but regrettably there is very often no really perceptible distinction between such religious communities and three or
four bachelors or working-girls sharing an apartment. It goes without saying that there is a difference in motivation between the two
groupings. The religious are striving to form community, but the
working-girls live together for protection and because it saves
money. Inner attitudes, however, have no witness value. They
acquire such value only when they are made tangible in a mode of
life. In terms of poverty, this means that the dependence of each
on the group must be genuine and manifest. In other words,
personal possessions must be reduced to the minimum, and sacrifices must be made to hold as much as possible in common. 'As
much as possible' are the operative words here, because it would
be futile to attempt to go into detail. This is a matter for the
conscience of each, and the limits of possibility adopted in any
given group can be taken as a fair indication of the degree of
commitment.

The standard of living of religious communities poses a much
more delicate problem, because of the complexity of peoples'
reactions. The underprivileged condemn the wealthy, but they
also desire the same standard of comfort. Envy may condemn a
sister for returning home to a comfortable residence, but will the
sister or her community command respect and admiration by living
on the same level as the poor who resent their condition? I personally don't think so. Simply to share their misery does not help the
poor, and in addition we have already seen that a life of misery is
not in any sense an evangelical virtue. The poor may eventually
come to the realization that a group of religious share their standard of living because of love for them, and it is because of this
that there is a certain lack of clarity on this point. If the poor come
to respect and admire a religious community in their midst, it is
because they have been drawn into the reciprocity of dependence
and productivity that characterizes the vow of poverty of the
community. They are working together towards something better.

Merely to stand by and be poor says nothing. Not only is there no witness, but there may be the exact reverse. Respect is an essential ingredient of witness, and there can be no genuine respect where there is an element of fake. The poor may lack education but they are not unperceptive. They know that religious have the intelligence, the education, and the contacts to ensure themselves a comfortable living. Their first reaction to a group of religious living at their standard is one of suspicion. They suspect that they are being condescended to, that some sort of silly game is in progress at their expense. And this response will remain until it is modified by an appreciation of the quality of the motivation behind such a gesture. All of which goes to show that the gesture in itself has no impact, and therefore no witness-value. Living in a slum is just as bad as institutionalized charity in the sense that the individual or a group hides behind a material gesture. Paradoxically, it is the easy way out.

The above line of argument would appear to indicate that religious should live at the level to which their talents, industry, and good management entitle them. Nothing could be further from the truth. In a world where wealth is so unequally divided, scandal is not always pharisaical. Excessive wealth, however, must be judged, not in the abstract, but by the standards of the environment. What would be excessive in a developing country, and therefore a source of scandal, might not be so in a developed country. Even within a country regions differ, and a uniform monetary ceiling cannot be applied. Leaving aside the self-evident truth that religious are bound to give in charity, it seems possible, however, to suggest one generic criterion. This is suggested by the reciprocity that is the essence of the vow of poverty. It is wrong for a community to live exclusively, or almost exclusively, from the fruits of inherited capital. Not only is this a characteristic of the very rich in contemporary society, but it means that while the members live from the community they contribute nothing to it. Such a community, therefore, cannot mirror the Church of Jerusalem which is traditionally taken as the standard of religious life. Such a community may give much in charity, but that is beside the point; it has nothing to do with the vow of poverty. The religious is committed to giving himself. His charity may satisfy a material need of others, but it is meaningless in terms of witness value unless that money is born of his fatigue and labour.

I have stressed that witness demands visibility, and that the essence of the vow of poverty is sharing. It follows, therefore, that the sharing must be visible. In other words, no witness is given if outsiders are simply *told* that the members of a community have a vow of poverty. They must *see* the living out of the vow. This has very significant implications for the life-style of a community that is serious about giving Christian witness on the level of material possessions, because it means that such a community cannot afford to erect the barriers that have surrounded communities in the past. The degree of privacy that, in the past, was accepted as natural can no longer be maintained. If outsiders are to know where the money comes from and where it goes, and if they are to be able to see the sharing, then a community cannot isolate itself in restricted areas to which only members have access. A community that exists to influence the world by the quality of its life cannot be closed. A community that is sincere in its commitment to witness should not expect a greater degree of privacy than a large happy family whose children have many friends. The children and their friends come and go, but there are rules to ensure that the family has time for itself. Nonetheless the visitors have adequate opportunity to see the sharing that is the well-spring of its happiness.

It is easy to anticipate that the immediate reaction to this demand for less privacy will be rejection. Reasons will be found to support this attitude, but if they are examined carefully they will be found to be the very reasons which explain the drop in vocations, and the failure of religious communities to exercise any genuine influence on their environment. Even the current discussion regarding the material standards of poverty indicates the root of the malaise that we all feel. At bottom we are afraid of the truth that the reality of witness consists in *the quality of community life,* and as a result we strive to create structures that will convey the message without involving us personally. Genuine love, the self-sacrificing love of Christ is palpable. It does not need material props, and it surmounts all the inadequacies of environment. The vow of poverty is intended as one facet of that love, and when we examine our consciences we should concentrate on that love which is the essential, rather than on the material circumstances which are no more than its setting.

Celibacy and community

Although a definite improvement on previous authoritative statements, what Vatican II has to say about religious celibacy is still far from satisfying, because it concentrates exclusively on what celibacy means for the individual religious. In *Perfectae caritatis,* no. 12, there is only a passing reference to community : 'Above all, everyone should remember – superiors especially – that chastity has stronger safeguards in a community where true fraternal love reigns among its members.' This statement carries the clear implication that community has no intrinsic relationship to celibacy; common-life is no more than a convenient way for an individual to live out his commitment. I don't believe that the Council intended this implication, and so the ambiguity of the statement demands an explanation. I suggest that the ambiguity was motivated by a desire not to draw too clear a distinction between the celibacy of the religious and that of the secular priest. A reading of the Council documents manifests that there is no substantial difference between what is said of priestly celibacy (*Optatam totius,* no. 10; *Presbyterorum ordinis,* no. 16) and of religious celibacy (*Perfectae caritatis,* no. 12), so that commentators feel free to use the data contained in all three texts in order to create a uniform synthesis. In this one can detect the intention not to play into the hands of those who opposed priestly celibacy. To stress the intrinsic relation between celibacy and community, it was thought, would have been to weaken the position of those who wanted to maintain priestly celibacy, a position already gravely compromised by the admission that there was no intrinsic relationship between priesthood and celibacy. Paradoxically, the reverse is in fact true, and one of the strongest arguments for priestly celibacy emerges from an analysis of his place in the parish community. It is not my intention to develop this point here, but what can be said can be inferred rather easily from what will be said regarding religious celibacy and community.

THE NEW TESTAMENT

The classical New Testament passage cited as the basis for the vocation to celibacy is Mt. 19:12.

There are eunuchs who have been so from birth, and there are
eunuchs who have been made eunuchs by men, and there
are eunuchs who have made themselves unuchs for the sake
of the kingdom of heaven. He who is able to receive this, let
him receive it.

There is an allusion to this text at the very beginning of *Perfectae
caritatis*, no. 12. Fortunately the reference is very discreet, because
this passage has nothing to do with celibacy in the sense of the
decree. This statement, attributed to Jesus by Matthew alone, is in
response to the disciples' objection (19:10) occasioned by Jesus'
ruling that marriage after divorce is adultery (19:9 equals Mark
10:11-12). It must, therefore, be understood in the perspective of
the preceding discussion regarding marriage and divorce, and this
permits only one interpretation. The text concerns the fidelity that
is demanded of the abandoned partner in a marriage that has
broken up. Marriage is the total gift of self to another. The commitment is mutual, but the radicalism of Christian love means that if
one partner defaults the other is not freed. The totality of self-
giving means the acceptance of the possibility of throwing away
one's life for the other. This is accepted as entirely natural as long
as the two partners are faithful to each other, and history contains
many examples of husbands and wives who have willingly sacrificed
themselves for each other. Christian love is much more exigent, and
does not accept the faithlessness of one as sufficient justification for
the other to break the original commitment. It must continue
faithful, even when there is no human possibility of response. This
is the living death of the eunuch which the abandoned partner
must accept 'for the sake of the kingdom'. In other words, by
accepting enforced celibacy as the permanent possibility of return
and forgiveness for the sinner, the abandoned partner witnesses to
the altruistic character of Christian love, and manifests that he is
truly a follower of Christ who 'died for us when we were yet
sinners'. 'Why, one will hardly die for a just man, though perhaps
for a good man one will dare even to die. But God shows his love
for us in that while we were yet sinners Christ died for us' (Rom.
5:6-8). Thus, although Mt. 19:12 is not concerned with freely-
chosen celibacy, it says much about the radical character of genuinely Christian commitment in love.

It is in such radicalism that the New Testament roots of chosen
celibacy are to be discerned. Nothing more concrete or more specific

is to be found in the New Testament, but I think we can gain a valuable insight if we compare two texts which are not normally looked at together. Both appear in the gospel of Matthew :

> He who loves his father or mother more than me is not worthy of me; and he who loves son or daughter more than me is not worthy of me (10:37; cf. 19:29).
> And stretching out his hand towards his disciples, he said : Here are my mother and my brothers. For whoever does the will of my Father in heaven is my brother, and sister, and mother (12:49-50).

The first text appears in another form in Luke 14 :26, 'If any one comes to me and does not hate his own father and mother and *wife* and children and brothers and sisters, yes, and even his own life, he cannot be my disciple.' In biblical usage the 'hate' of Luke is equivalent in meaning to the 'love more' of Matthew. No mention is made of 'wife' in Matthew, and this accords with the above interpretation of the eunuch-saying. The fundamental message is identical in both, and is parallel to what Jesus said to the Rich Young Man. If affective ties interfere with commitment to Christ they must be abandoned. Were it not for the second text one might be tempted to infer from this that commitment to Christ could mean a life without affective bonds. Jesus, however, also makes it clear that commitment to him is the discovery of affective ties that did not hitherto exist. In the act of faith the believer becomes part of a community of love.

WHY CHOSEN CELIBACY?

Every Christian, however, is called to this renunciation and to this community. Yet not every Christian is called to voluntary celibacy. Why, then, are some so called? The only answer has to be inferred from the two texts juxtaposed above. The relationship of love that may have to be renounced is *different* from the relationship of love into which we enter with Christ, and the proclamation of the gospel demands that this difference be brought to the attention of the world. What precisely this difference is cannot be adequately specified in cold analytic categories, but this is irrelevant because the Christian is not asked to explain this new possibility of loving but to live it.

To love without adequate motivation, to love without hope of return, seems impossible to most men. They would like to believe because it would give immeasurably greater depth and richness to human life, but it appears as pure idealism, beautiful but completely impractical. They may be briefly inspired by an eloquent presentation of this ideal, but the only presentation that will really touch their hearts is the existential affirmation of this love in a consistent life-style.

By their baptism all Christians are called to give to the world this lived demonstration of the 'newness' of the love manifested by Christ. It is supposed to be their distinctive characteristic, both individually and collectively.

> A new commandment I give to you, that you love one another; even as I have loved you, that you also love one another. By this all men will know that you are my disciples, if you have love for one another (John 13:34-35).

What is new here is not simply the primacy given to the precept of charity, but the standard that is indicated. It must be a love as generous and as universal as the sacrificial love of Christ. The impact of such love has been well underlined by Tertullian's ironic remark : 'It is especially this exercise of charity that has given us a bad character in the eyes of many. See, they say, how they love one another! Because they [i.e. the pagans] hate one another. See, they say, how they are ready to die for each other! Because they [i.e. the pagans] are ready rather to kill each other' (*Apolog.*, 19:7). And Minutius Felix commented : 'They love each other even before they come to know each other' (*Octavius,* 9:2). Could a Christian apologist today, without ridicule, put the same observation in the mouth of an adversary?

Absolutely speaking, celibacy is not necessary to the existential demonstration of the 'newness' of Christian love. Married love is intended to extend to all others in the Christian community with the same intensity as is shown to members of the family. Theoretically, it is fully capable of having the same impact as celibate love. The operative word here is 'theoretically', because in the practical order the situation is very different, and it is on this level that witness is effective. Celibate love has a greater witness value than married love, because it is less ambiguous. Marriage is a natural institution, and love of great intensity and dedication can and does exist in marriages that make no claim to be Christian. The witness value of Christian married love, therefore, is diminished by the difficulty of distinguishing the natural from the genuinely Christian. In other words it is too easy to explain away. The outsider is not immediately impressed or disturbed by the presence of something 'new'. In certain cases the superhuman dimension of Christian married love may be inescapable, for example, in the fidelity and devotion shown to a partner who is a permanent invalid, but this is irrelevant in the perspective of a theology of witness which must of necessity concern itself with the ordinary case and with normal situations. This is not intended as a disparagement of married love. It is in no way inferior to celibate love. Christian marriage is rooted in the same faith and hope that inspires religious life. However, from the point of view of witness we have to place ourselves in the position of the outsider. Motives do not impinge on his perception unless a life-style translates them into the domain of sensible reality. Married love does this less effectively than celibate love simply because it permits more alternative explanations. The presence of a partner obscures the commitment to the ideal, because the outsider can find familiar explanations to account for such love, sex, companionship, support, etc.

The parish and the diocese are intended to be true communities, but each is made up of family units which in themselves are communities. The married Christian, therefore, of necessity belongs to *two* communities, the family and the local Church. In practice the edges of the distinction between the two are inevitably blurred, and no one can tell whether he is sustained by the natural love of the family or the 'new' love of the Christian community. In times of crisis the married Christian can move both consciously and unconsciously from one community to the other. When the Church fails him he can turn to the family, and when the family fails him to the Church. It is this fluidity that detracts from the witness value of married love, no matter how profoundly Christian it may be.

The celibate, on the other hand, belongs to only one community. In opposition to the parish, this microcosm of the Church is not made up of smaller communities, but of individuals. In this sense it is an ultimate community like the family, but it is not bound by any ties of blood. Since all the members are sexually normal adults of the same sex, the mere fact of its existence forces the mind of the outsider to seek the motivation for its existence. None of his normal standards of judgement apply. He cannot fit the religious community into any of his habitual categories. It is precisely because of its ability to produce this effect that the witness value of celibate love is superior to that of married love, because the essence of witness is to force outsiders off balance in such a way that they are obliged to ask the crucial question, 'What makes them different?' This is confirmed by the simple fact of experience that outsiders show much more curiosity about religious communities than about Christian marriages. I would even go so far as to say that the witness value of married love depends on the witness given by celibate love, in the sense that it is only when the outsider had been alerted by a celibate community to the 'newness' of Christian love that he can discern the much more subtle signs of this love in a Christian marriage.

CELIBACY AND COMMUNITY

Despite what has been said above it does not follow that every religious community gives greater witness than every Christian marriage. Some families are a much more effective proclamation of the gospel than many religious communities. The point that I have been making is that in itself celibate love has a greater witness potential than married love. Hence, it has a necessary function in the Christian community. Whether this potential is always effectively realized is a separate question to which we must now turn.

It is often said that in virtue of the vow of celibacy the religious is freed to love, and this theme is taken up by the Council documents when they speak of celibacy. With regard to religious the formulation is a little discreet, because it says only that celibacy is 'a most suitable way for religious to spend themselves readily in God's service and in works of the apostolate' (*Perfectae caritatis,* no. 12). This could mean a number of things, but the mind of the Council is clearly indicated in the passage concerning priestly celibacy, 'They more freely devote themselves in him and through him to the service of God and men' (*Presbyterorum ordinis,* no. 16). Such an understanding of celibacy not only ignores the realities of life, but is in conflict with the common-sense attitude of the traditional teaching on the hierarchy of charity. In maintaining that the primary obligation of charity concerns those who are closest to us St Thomas quotes both Paul and Augustine (II-II, q. 26). According to the former, 'If anyone does not provide for his relatives, and especially for his own family, he has denied the faith and is worse than an unbeliever' (1 Tim. 5:8). This idea is generalized by Augustine, 'Since it is impossible to be useful to all, you should give preference to those who are closest to you by reason of circumstances of time or place or for any other reason' (*Doct. Christ.*, I, 28). The religious is no freer than a married persion. If a husband or wife is limited by the concern he or she is obliged to manifest for his or her family, the religious is limited in precisely the same way by concern for the community. It is an unfortunate paradox, but the idea that celibacy frees for universal love is one of the major reasons why religious communities have failed to fulfil their witness potential, because inevitably this gives rise to the view that the community is merely a base *from which* the real work is done. The result is that religious communities become loveless deserts. Not only does this make celibacy virtually impossible because men cannot live without love, but it means that the outsider who is shocked into asking 'What makes them different?' finds nothing but a verbal answer to his question. The real answer, the existential answer, is lacking. Not unnaturally, then, celibate life is judged to be meaningless. If religious life produces shock as an immediate reaction, it must also appeal when it is looked into more deeply, and it does this only when the quality of life in a celibate community speaks to the buried desire of all men for totality and completeness.

Celibacy is but another facet of the reciprocity that we have seen to be characteristic of the vow of poverty. In poverty we give all to the community and receive all on the level of the means of material subsistence. Similarly in celibacy we give all to the community and receive all on the level of affective life. Just as the community meets our material needs, so it must also meet our affective needs. Just as the religious is productive in material terms, so he must also be productive in affective terms. These two areas cover the fundamental needs of humanity. Without bread and love man cannot live. Consequently there is a very profound reason why poverty and celibacy were chosen as the structural elements of religious life. They manifest, in the two domains with which all men must be concerned, the shared being-in-Christ which is the essence of Christian life. The fraternal charity that should animate common-life is not simply a safeguard for celibacy, it is an integral part of the witness that is given by celibacy.

COMMUNITY LIFE

We have seen that the *raison d'être* of celibacy is on the level of witness. It is not for the individual who is celibate, but for those who do not know the liberating power of Christian love. It is a sacrifice 'for the sake of the kingdom', not in the sense that it is an easier or sure way for the religious to attain the kingdom of God, but in the sense that the kingdom of God may be manifested as unambiguously as possible as a community in which men are loved not for what they are but for what they can become.

The real danger for celibates is not the build-up of a sexual tension that cannot be controlled, but the suppression or deflection of the affective powers. They are stifled if the celibate avoids the stress and tensions of deep interpersonal relations. In any religious community, no matter how committed and how sincere the members, there will be such tensions, because it is a formation-community in which perfection is only the goal striven for, not a condition of membership. We strive to be all 'spirit' but, as Paul was well aware, the 'flesh' is still active. Even in a community where all are sincerely striving to let the Spirit dominate, emotional tensions will accumulate to the point where a flash of passion is the inevitable result. Since a religious community is supposed to be a community of peace, the recurrence of such explosions worries many. Sometimes a guilt complex develops, and an attempt is made to eradicate the root of such tensions by withdrawal to a more superficial level of involvement in the community. The unfortunate result is that the personality becomes sterile, because its life is nothing more than a protective system of evasion and compromise. If this happens all the witness value of that life vanishes. It is not necessary that it should happen. It should be recognized that emotional tensions are a concomitant of human living, and that a good row between relatively mature individuals is a very healthy thing. It might help to recall that both Jesus in the episode of the money-changers in the Temple, and Paul in the Corinthian letters, discharged their inner tensions in passionate outbursts of extreme violence. In a formation-community an explosion of passion is an essential ingredient in conversion. Not only does it lead to deeper self-knowledge, but in the aftermath one sees new opportunities for love. Both Jesus and Paul compare Christians to 'children', and a small child is the only human being who reacts with instinctive honesty in interpersonal relations. What is praised in the child is this simplicity, not the lack of control that often accompanies it. Maturity is the acquisition of the necessary controls but care must be taken – and this is specially true of the celibate – that honesty remains intact. By any standards sincerity and honesty, both of which imply courage, are essential ingredients in a life capable of commanding respect and admiration.

The alternative to the suppression of affective powers is to permit them to be deflected, either to 'things' or to persons outside the community. The celibate's life can all too easily become centred on substitutes such as art, research, administration, a project. If one is successful the resulting acclaim can meet the need for affective love. Should this happen the reciprocity that is integral to the witness of celibacy is destroyed, because the member no longer lives *from* the affective life of the community. There is no lasting satisfaction in this way, and failure often reveals a trading mentality. Having, he thinks, given himself entirely to God, the religious feels that he is owed certain satisfactions. When these are not forthcoming, because the whole idea is false, bitterness and cynicism are the result. This phenomenon is frequent when community is conceived simply as a base, and celibacy is thought of in terms of service. Celibacy is certainly for service, not the service of *doing,* but the service of *loving.* Actions, of course, are involved, but the error lies in considering them as primary. The intensity of love with which they are infused is the only thing that really matters.

The witness value of celibacy is much less seriously weakened if the affective powers are focused on persons outside the community, because celibate love is obviously meant to overflow the rather narrow limits of a community. A danger for the witness value of celibacy arises only if and when the affective *centre* of the religious' life is displaced outside the community, because at that point he ceases to live from the community affectively, and the tangible evidence of the reciprocity of Christian being is destroyed. A second danger then becomes imminent. Psychic energy is limited, and it is naturally chanelled in a give-and-take relationship. If the affection needed to live humanly comes from outside the community, it is inevitable that the affective powers of the religious will also be chanelled in that direction, thus leaving the rest of the community less to live on. Psychic capital cannot be measured as accurately as money, but the analogy is not too remote. Unless all the members of the community produce to the limits of their affective capactiy, the quality of the community's life – which is its *raison d'être* – will diminish.

The most subtle way in which this can happen is the religious' involvement with the various generations of his own family. In itself such involvement is a good thing, because without such contacts the best of communities become claustrophobic, and it is a human need to be able to stand back at moments and look at community with the perspective given by distance and a point of comparison. The difficulties of family life are such as to provide a most effective deterrent to the idea that religious are the only group to have troubles and tensions. Moreover, an awareness of the roles being worked out in a family can permit a religious to detect infantile attitudes in what is supposed to be a community of mature adults. However, these (and many other) positive advantages, when reinforced by the claim of blood, can bring a religious to the point where he (or she) knows his nieces and nephews better than the youngest members of his community. At this point it is clear that more of himself (time, thought, energy) is being given to those outside than to those inside the community.

From a theological point of view the problem of friendship with a member of the opposite sex is identical with the problem of over-involvement with one's own family. It is governed by the same principle, and it carries the same built-in danger. Unfortunately, however, the danger implicit in this type of relationship is most often exaggerated to the point that such friendship is considered incompatible with celibacy. Such a reaction is one-sided, because this relationship has as many positive aspects as involvement with one's own family. Real maturity (which is indispensable to witness) demands that an individual be able to relate to both sexes. This ability cannot be acquired in a vacuum. It is also a fact of experience that individuals learn infinitely more about themselves through friendship with a member of the opposite sex than through contacts with their own sex. The former carries with it an intensity lacking in the latter because of the natural complementarity of the two sexes, and unless confronted with this intensity an individual can remain completely unaware of the strengths and weaknesses of his own character. In far too many communities the view prevails that celibacy is a precious jewel that has to be 'protected' from tarnishment, and as a result contact with the opposite sex is reduced to the minimum. This is particularly true of female communities. This view involves two completely erroneous assumptions, namely, that women are somehow weaker than men, and that witness is given simply by the fact of having taken a vow of celibacy. This latter assumption is but a facet of the effort, which I have already criticized, to shift the burden of witness from the personal to the institutional. Anyone who still accepts the former assumption would do well to read D. S. Bailey's *The Man-Woman Relation in Christian Thought* (London, 1959) in order to fully appreciate the absurdity of the only reasons theologians could find to support the hypothesis that women are inferior to men. Such 'protectionism' is a much greater impediment to the witness value of a celibate community than any excess in an individual relationship, because it keeps the members in a state of immaturity which diminishes the quality of their lives. Scandal will also be invoked as an argument against any friendship between religious of different sexes. Given the contemporary situation it is undeniable that there will be 'talk', but this does not mean that true scandal is given. The laity are so badly informed regarding the true nature of celibacy that such scandal can only be classed as 'pharisaical'. And traditionally the danger of pharisaic scandal is no impediment to a course of action. It is also a fact of experience that such 'talk' disappears when such friendships are accompanied, not by a leap over the wall, but by a marked improvement in the quality of community life. Once such a climate has been established individual excesses are understood to be nothing more than an error of judgement on the part of an immature individual. It must also be recognized that the hyper-critical attitude of some so-called Christians forces such friendships into channels that they would not normally take in an atmosphere permeated by genuinely Christian trust and understanding.

To sum up. Celibacy is not freedom from responsibilities. It is just as much a commitment to responsibility in community as is marriage. The communities, of course, are different, but that is the whole point. The *raison d'être* of the celibate community is that its reciprocal love should be so manifest as to inspire a similar self-sacrificing love in the family (where, for example, the natural bond is often sundered by the generation gap) and in the wider community made up of family units. The necessity for celibacy is the practical one of contemporary need. People want to be *shown*, not told, that a love unshadowed by any possibility of selfishness does result in a more human person. They need the demonstration that a community of love is possible among those who are bound by no

ties of blood. In choosing celibacy the religious assumes the responsibility of answering one of the most fundamental questions of
contemporary man.

Tension and community

What I have written in previous sections was designed to substan-
tiate my belief that religious life not only has a place in the contemporary world, but that it is structurally designed to be a response to
man's deepest desires. By showing how religious life fulfilled a
function that was effectively realized by no other group I was
endeavouring to give hope to those who had come to doubt the
value of their chosen way of life. Nonetheless it would be foolish
not to recognize that what I have written carries the danger of
producing the reverse effect, because it seems to demand a standard of perfection that might appear idealistic and impossible to
those who have had to struggle with the difficulties of community
living. They legitimately wonder if, despite all the good-will and
all the efforts, genuine community will ever emerge.

TENSION A GOOD

More often than not our sense of dissatisfaction with community
is rooted in the continuous tension. It peakes at times, and diminishes at others, but never disappears completely. It seems to grind
us down and to take all the savour out of life. We begin to feel
that we are not really living, and a state of perfect equilibrium
begins to appear as the greatest of all goods. Only when we have
achieved rest, without any pull or drive, will we be truly 'free'.
Without any pressure, it is up to us to choose the moment and
type of activity that suits us. All this seems eminently desirable
when life seems made up of stimuli to which we are forced to
react.

We may never have spelled it out this clearly to ourselves, but I
am convinced that this desire, be it conscious or unconscious, for a
tensionless state is at the root of much current dissatisfaction with
community life. If this is correct, something has to be done about
it. Two possibilities immediately suggest themselves. We should

strive to make community life tensionless, and then the problem becomes : how? Or we can leave community and look elsewhere, and then the problem becomes : where? Both reflection and experience say that no answer can be given to either of these questions, and this suggests a third possibility, namely, that tension is an inescapable element of the human condition, and must be turned to profit. This, I believe, is not only the sole realistic attitude, but the only Christian one.

A quotation from Dr Viktor Frankl is apposite here :

> Mental health is based on a certain degree of tension, the tension between what one has already achieved and what one still ought to accomplish, or the gap between what one is and what one should become. Such a tension is inherent in the human being, and therefore is indispensable to mental well-being. We should not, then, be hesitant about challenging man with a potential meaning for him to fulfil. It is only thus that we evoke his will to meaning from its state of latency. I consider it a dangerous misconception of mental hygiene to assume that what man needs in the first place is equilibrium, or as it is called in biology, 'homeostasis', i.e. a tensionless state. What man actually needs is not a tensionless state, but rather the struggling and striving for some goal worthy of him. What he needs is not the discharge of tension at any cost, but the call of a potential meaning waiting to be fulfilled by him (*Man's Search for Meaning*, New York, 1967, Part II, pp. 165-66).

Precisely the same idea was formulated more succinctly by Nietzsche when he said, 'He who has a *why* to live for, can bear almost any *how*.' Tension is not something that can be avoided, but it can be given meaning and value by conviction.

TENSION AND THE IDEAL

I have tried to show that religious life crystalizes an ideal so extensive in its implications that total response is demanded. It is a value that calls to what is best and deepest in man. Once we admit the appeal of such an ideal we are under pressure, because an ideal is always at war with the *status quo*. By revealing the imperfection of the present, the acceptance of an ideal condemns us to perpetual dissatisfaction, because the 'good' is always challenged by the 'better'. The greater the grip the ideal has upon us the greater will be the sensation of failure.

Complacent ease is not in itself an ideal. It can only be the consequence of possession of an ideal. In our contemporary world the complacently at ease are those who have no genuine ideal, because in the concrete their attitude manifests an entire lack of concern. The multitudinous needs of others exercise no pressure. No call to self-transcendence is heeded. In a word, lack of tension is possible only to the completely self-centred who consider themselves to have all that their hearts desire.

By definition, therefore, the Christian will live under tension. From the moment that he takes his vocation seriously, others become more important than himself, and he san say with Paul:

> There is the daily pressure on me of my anxiety for the Church [lit. all the Churches]. Who is weak and I am not weak? Who is made to fall and I am not indignant? (2 Cor. 11:28-29).

The apostle bore this burden because 'the love of Christ urges me on', and he perfectly describes the attitude that should be ours:

> Not that I ... am already perfect, but I press on to make it my own, because Jesus Christ has made me his own. I do not consider that I have made it my own, but one thing I do, forgetting what lies behind and straining forward to what lies ahead, I press on towards the goal for the sake of the prize of the upward call of God in Christ Jesus (Phil. 3:12-14).

All sincere Christians are subject to this fundamental stress between the real and the ideal, between what we are and what we should become. In community this stress is intensified, both because religious are more conscious of the ideal and because they are aware of their responsibility to make that ideal tangible for others. As the exemplar of Christian community religious should be perpetually discontent with the quality of their lives, both individually and collectively. Satisfaction with community life is the danger signal, not discontent.

What then of the joy that, according to Paul, should be characteristic of Christian life? In order to understand what Paul means by Christian joy, we must take seriously his other assertion that suffering is inextricably bound up with genuine Christian living. The only way to reconcile the two assertions is to see this joy, not as something personal, but as something in which we share. Our lives in imitation of the man-for-others is entirely at the service of others. When we contribute something to them, they rejoice. And we share in that joy. We rejoice, not in what we have, but in the effect of what we have given.

INDIVIDUAL AND COMMUNITY

If we abstract from the special problem of incompatible personalities, the prime source of tension in religious life is the interaction of the individual with the community, and this is a problem that touches directly on the question of the quality of community life. The problem is posed today more acutely than ever before, because religious quite rightly are no longer disposed to suppress the natural human need to be needed *as a unique individual.* In the past religious were treated as anonymous and interchangeable cogs in the apostolate of the community, and God alone knows the price that was paid in unreasonable, unnecessary suffering. Superiors considered the task as much more important than the individual, and if square pegs had to be hammered into round holes, then such was the will of God! The younger religious of today fortunately have the courage to reject this mockery, and we have seen that it reflects an erroneous understanding of the religious community as an action-oriented organization.

What people *do* by way of work, projects, etc. is irrelevant to the apostolic dimension of religious life. This apostolate, as I have tried to stress in various ways, is exercised in and through the quality of common-life. Any specific works of social benefit that members undertake, either individually or collectively, are entirely secondary. To condemn a member as disobedient or unloyal because he or she shows a preference for a type of activity that is not traditional in the community is, therefore, unreasonable. Of course, it is equally possible, and equally wrong, for a member to attach undue importance to a particular activity, i.e. to make it his or her *raison d'être.* In both cases we have that form of escapism which has brought religious life into disrepute. We know what we can *do,* and so we put all the emphasis on that, because we are not at all sure of what we *are,* and very often we are afraid even to think about it seriously.

Much of the unnecessary tension that exists in religious commu-

nities would disappear if all the members were agreed on the meaning of religious life. The actual situation is that members of a
community entered for all sorts of different reasons. Some entered
because they felt it to be a surer way to save their souls, some
because of the liturgical life, some because it offered the possibility
of a non-competitive life of study, some because they felt called to
a life of selfless service. Each of these motives at the time o'
entrance was supported by a theology of the religious life which
had no genuine roots in the New Testament and which, moreover,
has shown itself to be barren. That almost unbearable tensions
should result is hardly surprising, because – despite the undeniable
sincerity and devotion of individuals – the so-called community is
rooted in division. I do not think that any techniques can be
devised to resolve such tensions. They are only intensified by efforts
to engender community by means of structures. They will, however, disappear eventually if great care is exercised in the selection
of candidates. This may appear to be a ridiculous suggestion at a
moment when vocations are decreasing, but I see no other way.

In the examination of prospective members of the community
the emphasis should not be put on their moral and intellectual
qualifications, but on their *motive* for desiring admission. This, of
course, is already done, but normally the question is posed very
imprecisely. I would put the question in this form : which is your
first priority, or which do you consider more essential, (a) witness
through the quality of community life, or (b) an active apostolate?
It should be noted that this question is concerned with where the
candidate puts the *emphasis*. He is not offered a choice between
witness or an active apostolate, because the two are not incompatible. Any candidate who said that his first priority was an active
apostolate should be refused, because he will never seriously consider the community as anything more than a convenient base of
operations. He may make conscientious efforts to create a genuine
community atmosphere, but this attitude will always be in conflict
with his deep-seated desire to be out and doing things for people.

On the contrary, the candidate who considers witness through
the quality of common-life to be the essential, can indulge in the
most active of apostolates without any danger. Because his priorities
are correct he will instinctively infuse both common exercises and
his attitudes towards other members with the life-giving force
which engenders true community. Community is nothing more than
sharing on all levels. This is why it cannot be created by tech-

niques of togetherness. But if all the members desire above all else to share with each other, then it springs into being inexplicable and beautiful. What has been said above about poverty should be taken as sufficient indication that even those who give first priority to witness cannot sit around all day and think about giving witness. No Christian, moreover, can sit idly by when faced by ignorance and want. Members of the community will have to move outside and *do* things, but if their priorities are correct they will never fall into the error of considering such service as their *raison d'être* as religious. To return to community will be a delight, not an interruption in something more important. This attitude will betray itself in all sort of ways unknown to the religious, and it is precisely at this point that the quality of community life begins to become tangible. It is a palpable force that not only draws the religious back to the true source of his life, but which also attracts those who want to believe that men can be human and that they can live together in peace and love.

The 'raison d'etre' of religious life

E. J. FOX, S.D.B.

It is incorrect to assert, as does Fr Jerome Murphy-O'Connor, that what religious do is irrelevant to the apostolic dimension of religious life.

I have immensely enjoyed reading Father Jerome Murphy-O'Connor's presentation of his ideas on the nature of the religious life, with particular reference to the scriptures. There were a great many fine things in his treatment of this vast theme, things that were not merely stimulating but that one felt needed to be said, and with which one could heartily concur.

There is, however, one point on which I should like to take issue and it is his view of the whole *raison d'être* of religious life. His thinking on this matter forms, I am well aware, a basic premise to much of his subsequent material, and it may seem strange that I can express agreement with many of his conclusions about religious life, while objecting to his major premise. In reply to this objection two things can be said. Firstly, I am suggesting not that his premise is totally false but that it is only partly true; and a half-truth needs to be questioned. Secondly, even if the premise were wholly false, we know from logic that 'a conclusion, even a true conclusion, can follow from false premisses' – *ex falsis quaelibet sequitur conclusio, etiam vera.*

In his analysis of the nature of religious life Father Murphy-O'Connor distinguishes between two different types of community, the 'community of being' and the 'community of action', and these two types of community are set in opposition to each other: 'Opposed to the action-community is the community of being.'[1]

He continues his argument with the statement that the Church, as revealed in the New Testament, 'is not an action-community but a community of being'. Since 'the religious community is the

1. *Supra,* p. 18.

same type of community as the Church',[2] it clearly follows that it, too, is not an action-community but a community of being.

Let me admit at once that I can lay no claim to being a scripture scholar and so it would be presumptuous for me to pretend to examine the scriptural foundation for the claim that the Church is a community of being rather than one of action. Although it seems to me that scriptural evidence could be marshalled to prove that apostolic action is of the very essence of the Church, I shall leave that task to those more competent than I in the scriptural field. What I must question, however, is the validity of the antithesis set up between 'being' and 'action' in Father Murphy-O'Connor's study. Even simple logic suggests that we have here an example of incomplete disjunction : why should a religious community have to be *either* a community of being *or* an action-community? Why should the two be set necessarily in opposition? Could not a religious community be essentially both?

THE RELEVANCE OF WHAT RELIGIOUS DO

In the final section of his study, the part entitled 'Tension and Community', the writer draws a conclusion which is perfectly consistent with his earlier premise :

'What people *do* by way of work, projects, etc., is irrelevant to the apostolic dimension of religious life. This apostolate, as I have tried to stress in various ways, is exercised in and through the quality of common life. Any specific works of social benefit that members undertake, either individually or collectively, are entirely secondary.'[3]

That is a statement with which I cannot agree, for, if it is true, it makes nonsense of the constitutions and traditional spirituality of the religious society to which I belong, as well as of the life of the founder, St John Bosco.

If the above-quoted assertion were made only about certain religious orders, then it might stand unchallenged, because it does seem to be true of the contemplative, monastic and semi-monastic orders. Unfortunately it is made as a generalization about all religious, as such, and therefore as applicable also to all the congregations of apostolic religious. That it is so applicable is what I deny.

To accept such a blanket assertion would necessitate closing

2. p. 21.
3. p. 67. Italics as in original text.

one's eyes to a whole process of historical development within the religious life itself, a process which is merely part of the wider plan of redemption as it unfolds and evolves within and through the history of God's pilgrim people.

Vatican II, in its Decree on the Appropriate Renewal of the Religious Life, *Perfectae Caritatis,* itself took cognisance of the fact that religious life has undergone a profound evolution since its beginnings in the desert of the Thebaid. The decree is careful to distinguish quite distinct forms of religious life, for which it lays down norms that are equally distinct; norms which are valid for one form are not necessarily valid for all the others. It would certainly be foreign to the thinking of the decree to formulate a definition of religious life on the model of the life of the monastic or mendicant orders and then extrapolate it into the realm of the more-recent foundations of apostolic religious communities.

About these latter the decree makes a statement which is of the utmost importance, since it represents a definite development in the Church's thinking about the essence of religious life and removes, at a stroke, any false antithesis between 'being' and 'action'.

'There exist within the Church a great number of clerical and lay institutes devoted to various aspects of the apostolate . . .

'In such communities *the very nature of the religious life requires apostolic action and services,* since a sacred ministry and a special work of charity have been consigned to them by the Church and must be discharged in her name. Hence the entire religious life of the members of these communities should be penetrated by an apostolic spirit, as their entire apostolic activity should be animated by a religious spirit. Therefore, in order that members may above all respond to their vocation of following Christ and may serve Christ himself in his members, their apostolic activity should result from an intimate union with him.'[4]

Examining this statement I should first of all like to concede most readily that, in so far as it asserts that 'apostolic activity should result from an intimate union with him', that is, with Christ, it agrees with Father Murphy-O'Connor that the fruitfulness of all apostolic activity is dependent upon the quality of the apostle's relationship with Christ. It is hard to see, however, how this passage from *Perfectae Caritatis* could possibly be reconciled with the

4. *Perfectae Caritatis,* section 8. Text from Abbott, *The Documents of Vatican II,* p. 472. My italics.

blanket assertion that what religious, at least those of the active, apostolic life, do by way of work is irrelevant to the apostolic dimension of religious life. The decree states the quite opposite view that what such religious do, their apostolic action and services, is in their case of the very essence of the religious life.

The meaning and validity of this view of the apostolic religious community is borne out when one examines the actual genesis of many of these communities. The starting point for their founders was often a quite specific work to which they felt called; the idea of founding a religious congregation developed from this initial impulse as a means of giving their work greater diffusion and permanence. I am quite certain that an examination of the work of such founders as St Vincent de Paul, St Jean Baptiste de la Salle or of Mother Teresa would confirm this fact. Perhaps I shall be forgiven, however, if I choose instead the work of the founder best known to me, St John Bosco, who founded the Society to which I belong.

ST JOHN BOSCO AND THE SALESIANS

The first article of our constitutions proclaims our faith in the fact that St John Bosco was raised up by God to assist in a specific work in the Church, the salvation of youth; the second article reminds us that 'it is by fulfilling this mission, in imitation of Christ, that we shall find the path leading to holiness'. In other words, even our imitation of Christ is coloured by our particular mission : as our rule puts it : 'Reading the gospel we become sensitive, like Don Bosco, to certain aspects of Christ's personality, his gratitude to the Father for the divine call he gives to all, his predilection for the young and the poor. ... These are the gospel values which make our spiritual life and the apostolate come alive.'[5]

The life of our founder is the story of a growing awareness that God was calling him to a particular apostolate. Even as a boy he commented to his mother on the fact that priests, when they met him on the road, were cold and distant and never bothered to speak to him : 'If I am ever a priest, I won't be like that. I shall devote my whole life to young people. Children will never see me pass them by looking grave and distant. I shall always be the first to speak to them.'[6] The vivid and strangely-prophetic dreams

5. Salesian Constitutions, 41.
6. Suffray, *St John Bosco,* paperback edition, p. 22.

which he had from the age of nine onwards, in which he found himself being given the care of crowds of rough youngsters, were, if nothing more, clear indications that he felt his personal call to the service of Christ to be inseparably bound up with the care of the young.

Later, when he was a priest and beginning to help the poor boys who haunted the streets of Turin, he found that his rapidly-expanding work was more than he could cope with unaided. He accordingly tried to persuade some of his best boys to help him, and quite a number agreed to do so. Many of them, as soon as he had helped them in their education, left him; but a small nucleus remained faithful. There is a most illuminating entry in the diary kept at that time by Michael Rua.[7] He was then a boy in his teens and he records that on 26 January 1854 he and three of his teenage companions met in Don Bosco's room.

'It was proposed that we should begin, with the Lord's help, a period for the exercise of practical charity towards our neighbour. At the end of that period we might bind ourselves with a promise, and later on this promise might be changed into a vow. From that evening the name of Salesians was given to all those who adopted this kind of apostolate.'[8]

That handful of youngsters, brought together by the inspiration of Don Bosco's work on behalf of boys, was the nucleus of the future Salesian Society. There is a singular appropriateness in this simple account of the embryonic beginnings of the Society, because an essential feature of Don Bosco's whole approach to the ascetical life was that apostolic work, far from being irrelevant, was one of the principle constituents of the sanctity of an active religious. It is clear that the young founding members of the Society certainly considered that what specifically constituted them Salesians was 'this kind of apostolate'. The importance which Don Bosco attached to the apostolate is also reflected in the advice he once gave to the young Dominic Savio who had asked him how he could become a saint : 'The first advice Dominic was given to help him become a saint was to set out to win souls for God.'[9]

The same spiritual thinking was implicit in the words that Don Bosco often used as a form of greeting with his young Salesians :

7. Rua succeeded Don Bosco as superior general of the Salesians. He was beatified in 1972.
8. Auffray, *op. cit.*, p. 131.
9. John Bosco, *Life of Dominic Savio,* ed. T. O'Brien, s.d.b., p. 15.

'Salve! Salvando salvate.' This could be roughly translated as, 'Hullo! Make your own salvation sure by saving other people.' It thus becomes clear that our renewed constitutions are faithful to the spirit of the founder when they assert that 'it is by fulfilling this mission (i.e. work on behalf of youth) . . . that we shall find the path leading to holiness'.

A detailed study of the origins of the Salesian Society makes it perfectly clear that, in the mind of the founder, the Society with its vow of obedience is nothing else but the formula to ensure the stable establishment of the apostolic work which he knew was God's will for him and which he shared with his first collaborators.[10] Indeed the particular nature of the mission entrusted to any apostolic religious congregation colours the entire life of the members, even in those aspects which seem most peculiarly 'religious'. To take but one example, both the style and the rhythm of Salesian community prayer is to some extent conditioned by the fact that our founder wanted us to spend as much of our free time as possible with our boys, since truly friendly, educative relationships can best be established through contacts made in periods of recreation. Readiness to give up one's time in this way was also meant to be one of our most fruitful sources of mortification.

It is hardly possible in the space of this article to develop this point further, but I should like to quote again from *Perfectae Caritatis,* in order to show that what I have been saying is contained in the decree itself : '. . . inasmuch as the religious life which is committed to apostolic works takes on many forms, a necessary diversity will have to distinguish its path to a suitable renewal, and members of the various communities will have to be sustained in living for Christ's service by means which are proper and fitting for themselves.'a[11] In other words, the very religious practices of those communities who are committed to apostolic work will need to be conditioned by the demands of that work.

THE QUALITY OF LIFE

I have devoted myself throughout this article to rebutting the assertion that the kind of work undertaken by an apostolic religious community is irrelevant. I hope, however, that it will not be supposed that, because I have disagreed with this part of Father

10. Cf. *Memorie Biografiche,* Torino, vol. 2, p. 299.
11. *Perfectae Caritatis,* section 8. Abbott, p. 472.

Murphy-O'Connor's thesis, I would also want to question the great importance he attaches to the quality of the life we live in our communities. On this point I can, in fact, only agree with him most emphatically and express the wish that the many perceptive observations that he makes will bear abundant fruit. It cannot but be true that, unless our communities are permeated by a truly Christian spirit, unless they are places where men and women can unfold and grow in the light of Christ's love and of their love for one another, then our witness and our apostolic fruitfulness will be seriously nullified.

St John Bosco would have been wholly in sympathy with the plea for warm, friendly relations between religious in an atmosphere that promotes true sharing at the deepest spiritual levels. To be convinced of this fact one need only read some of the advice which he gave to the members of his first missionary expedition to South America : 'Love one another, advise one another, correct one another, and do not be carried away by either rancour or envy. Let the good of one become the good of all, and let the troubles and sufferings of one be regarded as the troubles and sufferings of all; and let each one strive to banish or at least to mitigate the sorrows of the others.

The man who wrote that had little to learn about the quality of human relationships.

I am aware, too, that Father Murphy-O'Connor seems to cover himself in advance against the danger of criticism of the kind I have made by affirming, at the end of his discussion, that there is no incompatibility between witness and active apostolate.[12] As he himself quite rightly says, it is all a question of emphasis; and my objection has been precisely to the emphasis chosen by him. When, for example, he suggests that any prospective candidate for a religious community – and presumably this includes any candidate for apostolic religious societies – should be refused admission if his first priority is the active apostolate, the writer has surely misunderstood the nature of apostolic religious life. He also seems to have failed to take into account the theological developments reflected in the passages of *Perfectae Caritatis* which I have quoted in this article.

As I suggested at the beginning, if Father Murphy-O'Connor is right on this particular point that I have discussed, then it would appear that St John Bosco was wrong and was leading his religious

12. Cf. p. 68.

up a spiritual blind alley. It seems to me unlikely that such is the case. I should, therefore, like to give the last word to Don Bosco. In the spiritual testament to his sons which he composed shortly before his death, he wrote : 'The world will always welcome us as long as all our concern is for the underdeveloped peoples, for poor children and for those members of society most in danger. This is our real wealth which no-one can take from us. ... Let us never forget that we exist for poor and abandoned boys.'

Or, as our Special General Chapter of 1971 put it succinctly : 'The *raison d'être* of the Salesians in the Church is the salvation of the youth of the working classes.'[13]

13. Acts of the Special General Chapter of the Salesian Society, English edition, p. 117.

A reply to Father Fox

The charism of the founder

JEROME MURPHY-O'CONNOR, O.P.

The question 'What were we founded to do?' is not irrelevant. The way in which I expressed myself may have given the impression that it was; that is my fault and I apologise.

Father Fox's article is a magnificent example of the type of response which I hoped my articles would provoke. The effort at sympathetic understanding, the care to give credit where it is due, and the closely-reasoned clarity with which an opposing view is expressed all contribute to making it a model of genuine dialogue in which both parties are enlightened. The difficulty he raises is a real one, as I know from many conversations with religious over the course of the summer, and so I feel an obligation to try and express myself a little more adequately.

There is a certain ambiguity in the idea of an 'action-community' because it can be understood either as (a) a community which *in fact* engages in activity or as (b) a community which is formed precisely in order to do things. I maintained that a religious community is an action-community in the first sense, but not in the second. It is precisely here that Father Fox (and many other religious whose communities were founded about the same time) beg to differ, because his congregation was founded in order to engage in a specific form of apostolic activity, namely, the salvation of youth.

He concedes that what I say does seem to be true of congregations founded before the Reformation, but goes on to deny its applicability to congregations founded thereafter because of 'historical development within the religious life itself'. Implicit in what he says is the belief that this development (whose reality I do not deny) is a good thing. I do not agree, because the effect of this development was to further obscure the distinction between 'the religious' and 'the Christian'.

CARELESS LANGUAGE

The distinction is often lost sight of because of the careless way in which language is used. Every Christian is in a sense 'religious', i.e. he is a person for whom religion is important. Equally every 'religious' is also a Christian. These statements clearly reveal that 'religious' is used in two distinct senses. In one case it connotes an attitude towards religion possessed by every true Christian, while in the other it connotes one who has committed himself or herself to a particular modality of the Christian life, namely, life in a community composed of members of the same sex. Everyday speech clearly distinguishes between 'a religious person' and 'a religious'. Because religious life is a special modality of the Christian life, as the special treatment accorded it by the Council indicates, there must be an adequate distinction between the two.

'PERFECTAE CARITATIS' (no. 8)

At this point I must turn to *Perfectae Caritatis,* section 8, because I do not find it as satisfactory as Father Fox does. It is not that I disagree with what is said, but I discern an ambiguity that seems to have escaped him. I myself may even be responsible for this, because my articles also contained an ambiguity which I hope to dissipate.

According to this Council document 'the entire religious life of the members of these communities should be penetrated by the apostolic spirit, as their entire apostolic activity should be animated by a religious spirit'. It should be noted first of all that this text does not speak of community as such, but of *the members* of these communities'. It is concerned, therefore, with the individuals who constitute such communities. When these are taken precisely in their individuality it can only be question of their Christian vocation. This interpretation is confirmed by the next sentence of the document which speaks of 'their vocation of following Christ [to] serve Christ in his members'. Here it is question of the vocation of all Christians who in virtue of their baptismal consecration are committed to the following of Christ and to the service of Christ in his members. For the New Testament there is only one way of following Christ, namely, total commitment to his person generating a love which puts one completely at the service of others. The New Testament does not permit any choice in the degree of commitment. Total, radical dedication of one's entire self is expected of those who have responded to the call of God in Christ. The lives of all Christians, therefore, were intended to be 'apostolic', because so was the life of Christ, and this apostolate will evidently be animated by 'a religious spirit' because it is rooted in union with Christ. Hence, it can be misleading to say, as the Council document does, that 'the very nature of the religious life requires apostolic action and service' – misleading unless one remembers that this is first of all true of the nature of Christianity itself. The statement in *Perfectae Caritatis* is true only because those who become religious do not thereby cease to be Christians. All the demands of their Christian vocation remain unchanged. Intrinsic to their commitment to Christ through faith and baptism is the obligation to serve Christ in his members. The practical implication of this is that *every* Christian *must* be actively concerned about the plight of the sick, the poor, the underprivileged. Once again, this is not a matter of choice. The terrible judgement scene in Matthew 25:31-46 formally teaches that Christians will be damned for their lack of concern.

In this perspective, let us now look at the situation obtaining at the time when many religious communities were founded in order to meet specific social needs, notably the care of the sick and the education of youth. According to the gospels such needs are the concern of all Christians. Many, however, refused to meet this demand of their Christian vocation, but there were the few who saw what the love of God in Christ demanded and rose to meet the challenge. The call to serve the sick or to educate youth is not a special vocation. It is an integral part of the Christian vocation, as the parable of the Good Samaritan teaches. The fact that some heeded this call at a time when a supposedly Christian society ignored it proves only that there were some genuine Christians around.

SOME FOUNDED LAY ASSOCIATIONS, OTHERS RELIGIOUS CONGREGATIONS

In a sense it is only natural that those Christians who saw the need should have banded together for mutual support in the face of the apathy of the majority, but it is not without profound significance that two specifically different types of group arose. On the one hand, there were the religious congregations such as the Salesians, and on the other, the lay associations such as the Society of St Vincent de Paul.[1] In terms of the specific apostolic work done there is no difference between the Salesians and the Society of St Vincent de Paul. As Father Fox informs us, 'The *raison d'être* of the Salesians in the Church is the salvation of the youth of the working Classes.' The Society of St Vincent de Paul 'was founded in order to sustain young people in the faith by the practice of charity'.[2] Both organizations, therefore, were founded for the salvation of youth. Yet there is a difference, as both the Church and the members of the two organizations have always recognized.

In what does the difference consist? It would be as invidious to place the distinction on the level of dedication of individual members as it would be to compare the sanctity of Don Bosco with that of Frédéric Oznam. One presumes that some Salesians are more dedicated than some members of the Society of St Vincent de Paul, but equally that some members of the Society of St Vincent de Paul are more dedicated than some Salesians. It should go without saying that I am speaking of genuine dedication shown in active

1. The Society of St Vincent de Paul is perhaps the best known of the charitable organizations, but there were many others. Cf. *The New Catholic Encyclopaedia*, Index under 'Charitable Organizations', and A. Vidler, *A Century of Social Catholicism 1820-1920* (London, 1969).
2. A. Vidler, *op. cit.*, p. 24.

concern and not of theoretical commitment. If a difference is to be found it can only be sought on the level of the inspiration of the founder. The spark of this inspiration was certainly a social need to be met by apostolic work. Yet one founded a religious community under vows and the other a lay association. One bound his followers to something much deeper than the other. There is no necessary connection between this added depth and the work to be done. Hence, in addition to the call of God manifested in a specific need one is obliged to postulate a special impulse of the Spirit whose full implications Don Bosco may not have explicitly recognized because he was as much a man of his time as we are of ours.

In examining the inspiration of their founders it is not sufficient for religious congregations simply to look at the social need that they were founded to meet, because such needs should call forth a response in every Christian. They must face squarely and honestly the fact that, confronted with the same needs, other totally dedicated Christians, reacted by forming social units that are not the same as religious communities. In consequence, what Don Bosco (to take but one example) *did* indicates to me his instinctive understanding of the importance of full community. Therefore, any investigation of the charism of a founder must be a quest for ways to bring this latent awareness to explicit expression. Under the guidance of the Spirit the founder (or foundress) of a religious congregation, whether consciously or not, intended to do *something more* than merely meet a social need. The primary question that religious must ask themselves, therefore, is not 'What were we founded to do?' but 'Why were we given this particular form of life?'

ACTIVITY NOT IRRELEVANT

The question 'What were we founded to do?' is not irrelevant. The way in which I expressed myself in my essay may have given the impression that it was; that is my fault and I apologize. Father Fox, therefore, is entirely correct in criticizing my statement that 'What people do by way of work, projects, etc., is irrelevant to the apostolic dimension of religious life.' If the social need discerned by the founder is still not being adequately met by other Christian organizations, then the members of that community remain obligated to meet that need. Meeting such a need is a valuable and necessary form of the apostolate. It should be remembered, however, that this obligation devolves on them not in virtue of their commitment to a particular congregation, but in virtue of their baptismal commitment to Christ. Their relationship to a particular founder serves as a catalyst to sensitize them to a particular need.

In writing as I did I had two particular concerns in mind, both of which obscured my view of the aspect treated in the previous paragraph. The first was the situation of religious congregations that are being forced out of their traditional apostolates. I intended to console them by emphasizing that the precise work in which they were engaged was not the most important dimension of their religious life, and that in consequence they could move to a different apostolate without destroying themselves. When I wrote as I did I was concentrating exclusively on the idea that the fundamental and proper apostolate of a religious community was the witness value of its corporate life. Now, due to Father Fox's prompting, I see that there is another dimension which is but an aspect of the founder's charism. None of the founders or foundresses took on works that they felt were being adequately handled already. Hence, the charism of the founder or foundress would seem to indicate that we move out of areas where we are not really needed. However, since the charism of our particular foundation sensitizes us to special areas of need, it will prompt us to respond to needs closely associated with the original problem which evoked the founder's authentic Christian response. Thus, those in hospitals would consider the need for preventative medicine in the homes of the poor, and those in education would consider the demand for remedial teaching.

My second concern was with situations where the original end of the congregation has been limited through custom. In some congregations the original apostolate (in the sense of the work done) of the founder has been arbitrarily limited by uncritical submission to various combinations of historical circumstances. Thus, for example, some congregations are committed to education of youth, but by tradition this has come to mean primary and/or secondary education. In practice this means that obstacles are put in the way of those who see the needs in third-level education, because they are not doing the 'normal' work of the congregation. In such situations this opposition must be critically evaluated. Does it have its roots in unthinking habit, or is it intimately related to the founder's charismatic insight? If the founder's view is in fact broader than the traditional interpretation, then individual members of the congregation have every right *to return* to the original inspiration.

The net result of all this should be to underline how fundamentally I am in accord both with *Perfectae Caritatis* and with Father Fox in their stress that religious must necessarily engage in apostolic work. The needs of the present are so great that no Christian can afford to stand aside, least of all religious whose commitment to Christ is so much more explicit than that of the rest of the laity.[3] We cannot just sit around and *be* religious however much we stress the primacy of the existential witness of community.

APOSTOLATE AND COMMUNITY

This, however, brings me back to Father Fox's key question : 'Why should a religious community have to be *either* a community of being *or* an action-community? Why should the two be set necessarily in opposition? Could not a religious community be essentially both?' In the light of what I have been saying it should be clear that I consider that a religious community is necessarily both, but it should be equally clear that I refuse to derive both facets from the same root. In reacting with concern to manifest social needs the members of a religious community are living out their Christian vocation. Without commitment in action that vocation would be merely a theoretical ideal, not a lived reality. Nonetheless, in addition to their Christian vocation religious have recieved another vocation. They have been called by God to assume the responsibility of demonstrating to the world by means of the quality of their corporate life the horizontal dimension of God's reconciling love in Christ. Thus, on the level of theory there is no contradiction or even tension between the religious community as a community of being and as an action-community. And both aspects, as I have indicated, can be traced to the charism of the founder or foundress.

3. Here, for the sake of clarity, I should perhaps once again emphasize that religious as such do not belong to the hierarchy of the Church. Theologically they are part of the laity, and it is accidental that some religious are also priests.

It is undeniable, however, that tension does develop on the level of practice, that is, on the level on which individual religious understand themselves and their communities. In actual fact, religious tend to be unaware of the specific modality that their religious vocation has added to their Christian vocation. It is difficult to discern why this should be so, but perhaps one suggestion could be made.

Given the understanding of obedience that has obtained in religious life up to the present it seems to me inevitable that the two aspects should have been confused, and that the most obvious should have assumed the primacy. The reason for this is that a genuine Christian response to need on the part of the individual religious had to be legitimized by the formal approval of the superior. This drew the individual's response, which was only the actualization of his or her Christian vocation, within the institutionalized structure of religious life. In itself this does not have much importance, but it had far-reaching implications for the psychology of the individual religious. From the fact that his or her apostolic activity had to have the approval of the superior who represented the community it was inferred that in such activity the individual represented the community. Thus, the idea gained currency that the apostolate of the community as such was exercised through the individual religious. Naturally enough this understanding of religious life was reinforced by what was only a partial grasp of the charism of the founder or foundress.

HAS COMMUNITY APOSTOLIC VALUE?

My real quarrel with this development is not simply that issues have been obscured, but that in the process a crucial element has been lost sight of, namely, the one element which sets religious apart from the laity and which is their life together in a particular form of community. Little or no attention has been devoted to the question : Has community as such (i.e. apart from the apostolic work of individual religious) any apostolic value? *Perfectae Caritatis*, for example, ignores this point completely.

Many of those who consider the question do answer in the affirmative. Yes, they say, our community runs a school in which we all teach, or runs a hospital in which we all work. At first sight this seems an adequate answer to the question, because the apostolate is at the level of the community. This, however, is a dangerously deceptive simplicity as even a brief examination will reveal. To educate the ignorant is a demand of the Christian vocation, and that fact does not change even when the number of Christians involved in the task is multiplied because of the advantages of co-operative effort. Take, for example a situation where a number of committed Christians are deeply concerned about the quality of education in their area. As a remedy they start a private lay school in which they all assume active responsibilities. How does this differ from a school run by religious? There is no difference from the point of view of education in its multiple aspects. Dedicated Christian lay teachers communicate just as much by way of Christian values as dedicated individual religious. Yet there is a difference. A co-operative Christian effort is not the same as a community. Those lay people who set up the school do not think of themselves as a community, but religious in the light of the inspiration of their founder do. Hence, we have to recognize that a community can operate on *two levels* in terms of apostolic service. One level is that proper to it as a religious community, and this apostolate is the existential witness given by the quality of its corporate life. The other level is that of the Christian vocation where the concern is with specific social needs. Some of these may be too great to be handled by a single individual, and in such cases the members of the community act co-operatively.

These distinctions may seem pedantic and redolent of an outdated scholasticism, but experience has shown that to ignore them is to make it impossible for individuals to change their attitudes. Religious must understand themselves, and understand the factors that have made them what they are if they are to truly see and appreciate the tremendous values that religious life contains. If they are to move in freedom in the new wind sweeping the Church and not to break in what to them is a frightening storm they must recognize that they have a double vocation. Their religious vocation does not cancel or stifle their Christian vocation. One presupposes and builds on the other. Even more, one is impossible without the other. Nonetheless, both involve *different* responsibilities, and one cannot be emphasized at the expense of the other. The operative phrase here is 'at the expense of', because this seems to be the impression that Father Fox gained from my articles, I still maintain, however, that some emphasis is necessary, if only to counteract false influences in the past. And so I would place the primary emphasis on the witness value of a community of being because that, after all is said, is what is specific of religious life.

Is scripture sufficient?

HENRY E. PEEL, O.P.

The active apostolate is not 'entirely secondary' in active religious orders ... The basis of Father Murphy-O'Connor's distinction bètween community of being and community of action is not self-evident.

Reading Jerome Murphy-O'Connor's reflections on the religious life (SUPPLEMENT, May-June 1973) I was reminded of the remark of Aelred of Reivaulx : 'Sitting with the brethren in a loving circle ... I found no one in that great circle whom I did not love and whom I did not believe loved me.' I suppose that everyone would agree that this expresses the *raison d'être* of religious life. The same idea has been expressed more abstractly in the statement that the purpose of religious life is the perfection of charity. Charity, of course, begins at home and the home for a religious is the community in which he lives. I don't think anyone would quarrel with that. Some of us, however, may be grateful for being reminded of it from time to time. It is very easy to be deceived into believing that involvement in the works of charity is the same thing as being charitable. The acid test is the quality of one's life and for a religious, living in community, this means primarily the quality of one's life in community, just as, for a family man, this means the quality of his family life. No involvement in apostolic action, however worthy, can be a substitute for this.

This being granted, however, we appear to be saying nothing more than that the *raison d'être* of religious life is to be as perfectly Christian as one can be. If we restrict ourselves to this generic level, leaving out of consideration the question of the means we take to achieve this perfection, one might legitimately conclude that the justification of religious life is that it is a manifest sign of the reconciliation of all men in Christ. This, in fact, is the conclusion arrived at by Father Murphy-O'Connor : 'The *raison d'être* of a religious community consists in the witness value of its corporate existence' (*ibid.*, p. 30). One might, perhaps, express the same idea by saying that the religious community is a specific way of making the Church visibly present in the world.

This is, indeed, one of the themes to be found in the theology of the religious life : 'The ecclesial significance of monachism is simply to live fully the holy, loving and praying life of the Church' (A. de Vogue, 'Monasticism and the Church in Cassian', quoted in Francois Vanderbroucke, *Why Monks?*, Cistercian Studies, 1972). The model of the religious life from this particular viewpoint is the picture of the primitive Church in Jerusalem as given to us by St Luke (Acts 2 :44-47). It is probable indeed that St Luke's picture is an idealized one. But, quite certainly, the idea of a primitive perfection is one of the recurring themes in the history of the religious life. The various movements based on the ideal of a return to the apostolic life which are a feature of the twelfth and thirteenth centuries were inspired by this ideal.

COMPLEX EVOLUTION

But there are many other themes in the complex evolution of the reality which we call the religious life. All of them are based on evangelical themes but it would be impossible to reduce them to a few texts of scripture : 'No religious order is the same as any other. If we were only to go to the New Testament we might miss the point of each of them. Each order is an attempt to live the perfect Christian life, but with special emphases on this or that' (Columba Cary-Elwes, o.s.b., *Monastic Renewal,* p. 62, Herder and Herder, 1967).

Every religious community is in some sense a particular way of making the Church present as a community of Christian love. But there are varieties of ways of doing this. The eremitical way of life can be lived in community but it is a community of solitaries. They share the same way of life but they share it in silence and solitude. The specific characteristic of this way of life can hardly be said to be 'participation in a common life'. It is that indeed but its distinctive feature is that it is eremitical. It witnesses in a most striking fashion to the final destiny of the Church – the contemplation of the eternal God.

St Benedict, who has some claim to the title of father of religious life in the West, was evidently convinced that the common life was, in general, a safer school of perfection than withdrawal into solitude. In passing, it may be remarked that to enter a school does not make one a scholar. But it can scarcely be denied that religious life is deliberately designed as a school of perfection. Nothing further is intended by the use of the phrase 'state of perfection'. If it is a form of 'elitism' to study the science of the saints it would seem that this form of 'elitism' is endemic to Christianity. We may take comfort, however, in the thought that the successful scholars at this particular school are totally unaware of their success. They regard themselves as most unworthy servants of their Master and of all those whom he loves.

I am not sure if the common life as envisaged by St Benedict and by all those who have adopted its basic pattern is the same reality as 'community life' as the term is used today. The major preoccupation with 'community' today appears to be at the level of human relationships. There is a search for greater informality, for ease in communication, for greater spontaneity and genuinely human friendship and understanding. In this religious life is simply reflecting the cultural environment in which we find ourselves today. None of us live in a spiritual vacuum, insulated against the prevailing pressures and hungers of humanity. To seek to do so might be good neo-Platonism but it would be very bad Christianity.

AN ORDERED COMMUNITY

St Benedict in his legislation sought to create a peaceful, ordered community. The peace of the community springs from the observance of the rule which orders the whole life of the monastery. Singularity in dress or behaviour is viewed as a divisive element. Equality is absolute. 'The eighth degree of humility is for a monk to do nothing except what is authorized by the common rule of the monastery or the example of his seniors' (Rule, c.7). St Benedict is reacting against the excesses of individualistic searches for sanctity which sometimes marred the eremitical tradition. But in any discussion of community life some consideration must be given to the elements which are objectively shared. If uniformity has been stressed at the expense of charity it is no less true that charity is greatly strained where there is little actual sharing in communal duties. The 'holy rule' may have, on occasion, obscured the gospel itself. But pure personal initiatives seem to be oddly at variance with the self-emptying which is a condition of charity and hence of community. The monastic tradition, with its calm objectivity and rituals of behaviour must have some elements of permanent value. It would scarcely have survived for so long otherwise.

Though the monastic life was not initially conceived with a view to a specific function within the Church or the world its influence nevertheless was profound and widespread in both spheres. Limiting ourselves simply to its 'witness' potential 'the monastic life as such, a life of the Spirit, a life of holiness, with its interior worship, is a proclamation of the kingdom of God already visible on earth. In this respect, our proclamation of faith is a work of the Spirit; it supposes a power of the Spirit bestowed upon us in Confirmation. It is also a proclamation of the transcendence and of the sovereign domain of God. Again it is a proclamation of the 'love' (*caritas, agape*) of God, descending upon men through Christ; and this *agape* becomes a visible reality in the monastic communion (*koinonia*) assembled in the Lord. It is also a proclamation of the gospel of poverty ...' (F. Vanderbroucke, *op. cit.*, p. 132). It is indeed possible to use the term '*koinonia*' as inclusive of all the realities which constitute the Church (cf. Jerome Hamer, o.p., *The Church is a Communion*, Geoffrey Chapman, London, 1964). It is equally possible to use the same term as descriptive of the religious life, which incarnates the Church in a special way. There is, however, a danger that the word 'community' might not convey the same meaning to the average reader as the word '*koinonia*' does to the scripture scholar or to the theologian.

The comparison may not be quite fair but I could not help recalling the battles between the friars and the secular masters in the University of Paris on reading Father Murphy-O'Connor's reflections on the active apostolate of religious. It seemed to me that he would side with the secular masters against Thomas Aquinas and Bonaventure. Religious should stay out of the schools and they should earn their living instead of being beggars. This was the brunt of the argument against the friars. This is hardly the place to fight that battle again. Those who are interested can consult the opusculum 'Contra impugnantes Dei cultum et Religionem'.

NOT ENTIRELY SECONDARY

The active apostolate of religious who belong to institutes devoted to different kinds of apostolic work is not something 'entirely secondary' (*supra*, p. 67). 'In all such institutes, apostolic and charitable activity is of the essence of religious life; for it is a holy service and work of love which is their own, entrusted to them by the Church and discharged in her name'

(*Perfectae Caritatis,* n. 8, translated by James Walsh in *Supplement to The Way,* May 1966, p. 34).

It is hard to see any justification for maintaining a religious institute in existence if it does not continue to embody the particular charism of its founder. It is equally hard to see how the particular charism of many religious founders is not the service of Christ in his members. The classical expression of this is, perhaps, the inspiration of St Vincent de Paul : 'You have for a monastery the houses of the sick; for a cell, your hired room; for a chapel, the parish church; for cloisters, the streets of the town; for an enclosure, obedience; for a grille, the fear of God; for a veil, holy modesty.'

The manifest emphasis of St Vincent de Paul is on the active apostolate of charity. The same is true of many other religious founders. To assign secondary importance to the specific work for which the institute was originally founded is to remove its *specific raison d'être.* The quality of community life will clearly be conditioned by the kind of activity which is the specific purpose of the institute.

It was the friars who linked the tradition of monastic religious life to the exercise of an active ministry. All the contemporary evidence points to the fact that this was the special charism of St Dominic. The preaching was not the 'witness potential of the community' but the proclamation by word of mouth. Because of this ministry St Dominic adapted the traditional observances of monastic life to the needs of the Church at the time. The *specific raison d'être* of the Dominicans is preaching. Because of this the power of dispensation was included as an integral part of monastic observance. This brilliant innovation ensured the necessary freedom for the ministry within the structure of common life. The primitive constitutions of the order made this point with the utmost clarity. The passage merits quotation :

Because a precept of our rule commands us to have one heart and one mind in the Lord, it is fitting that we who live under one rule and under the vow of one profession, may be found uniform in the observance of canonical religious life, in order that the uniformity maintained in our external conduct may foster and indicate the unity which should be present interiorly in our hearts. This will be able to be achieved more readily and more completely and kept in the forefront of our memory, if the things which we are obliged to do are committed to

writing; if the manner in which we are supposed to live is
made known to everyone in writing; if no one may change or
add or subtract anything on his own authority; lest through
neglect of the smallest detail we gradually fall away. For this
reason, however, the prelate shall have power to dispense the
brethren in his priory when it shall seem expedient to him,
especially in those things which are seen to impede study,
preaching, or the good of souls, since it is known that our order
was founded, from the beginning, especially for preaching and
the salvation of souls (edited by Francis C. Lehner, o.p., *Saint
Dominic, biographical documents,* The Thomist Press, Wash-
ington, 1964).

DISTINCTION NOT CLEAR

The basis of the distinction between an 'action community' and a
'community of being' which Father Murphy-O'Connor uses in his
interpretation of religious authority and obedience is not self-
evident. Every example limps but the fitness cult as practised in a
health club and the search for the charity of Christ which is
sought by those who enter religious life do not seem, even remotely,
comparable. The image clouds the issues rather than clarifies them.
'Being' and 'doing' cannot be divided so neatly. Our behaviour
moulds our personality. There are tasks to be done and it is the
responsibility of authority to assign people to do them.

The older monastic tradition continued to live in the new form
of religious life which the friars inaugurated. The emphasis on
common life, so characteristic of Benedictine spirituality, remains a
living force. The recurrent phrase 'faithful to choir and refectory'
in Dominican hagiography highlights this emphasis. But there is an
equally obvious shift of emphasis in the fact that study replaces
manual labour and in the regulation that : 'All the hours are to be
said in church, briefly and succinctly lest the brethren lose devotion and their study be in any way impeded.'

This type of religious life produced a characteristic type of
spirituality. It was basically contemplative, centred on communal
liturgical celebration and orientated outwards towards God and the
needs of one's neighbour. Community life was a sharing in objec-
tive aims and ideals. It was less concerned with personal relationships than with the foundations on which these are built. Because
man is conceived as a unity there is great emphasis on bodily

gesture, ritual and ceremonial. Bodily gestures and the use of the voice enter into the worship of God and they are conceived as an integral part of religious life. There is a certain lack of haste; a leisurely movement; a contemplative spirit. There is an atmosphere of calm objectivity and little preoccupation with self except in relation to God and one's neighbour. Community meant being of one mind and one heart in the Lord.

The prototype of the active religious institutes which proliferated after the sixteenth century is the Society of Jesus. Their spirit inspired many other religious institutes both by their example and by their influence as confessors and spiritual directors. It is with the Jesuits that the analogy of the Church as a military organization 'one of the most pernicious ideas ever introduced into Christian theology'! (supra, p. 17), truly religious life.

I think one can safely generalize and describe the new religious spirit as a shift away from external community observance to internal, personal discipline. Personal prayer in silence replaces the choral chanting of the Divine Office. There is a movement away from the embodiment of religion in externals to inward discipline and techniques of private meditation. The religious habit disappears to be replaced by the clerical garb of the time and place. Cloister is abandoned. Monastic disciplines of fasting and bodily austerity are replaced by a more rigid discipline of the will. There is greater introspection; more self-examination; the technique of the particular examen; severe scrutiny of motives and intentions. Combined with this there is a much harsher discipline of obedience. The Jesuits were a disciplined, mobile force, totally at the disposition of the Church in the person of the Pope, to be employed anywhere.

JESUITS IN EDUCATION

The atmosphere in which this new religious spirit originated was, of course, the atmosphere of the Counter-Reformation. There is a prevailing atmosphere of being geared for action. These new religious are to be found everywhere but, perhaps, their greatest single achievement is in the field of education both lay and clerical. Here the Jesuits were the vanguard. Many of the new seminaries, the creation of the Council of Trent, were staffed by them. They went into the universities. They founded their own schools. St Ignatius once noted that the safety of the faith depended 'much less on preachers than on teachers'. The Catholic school, managed and staffed by religious emerged and a whole new philosophy of Catholic education evolved. The Jesuits drew up their own plan of studies, integrating the new humanist culture of the Renaissance into their system. The system was wonderfully successful. The Protestant Francis Bacon wrote concerning it : 'As for the pedagogical part the shortest rule would be, Consult the schools of the Jesuits; for nothing better has been put into practice' (Michael Foss, *The Founding of the Jesuits,* Hamish Hamilton, London, 1969, p. 166).

The Jesuit involvement in secular education provoked opposition, even from within their own ranks. One Jesuit wrote : 'Boys are by nature giddy, restless, talkative and lazy creatures, so that even their parents cannot control them at home. Therefore our young men who teach them lead a very hard life, fritter away their strength and lose their health' (*ibid.,* p. 164). There was an idea that highly-educated and dedicated Jesuits could be better employed than in teaching secular disciplines to growing boys. But the involvement became part of the Jesuit tradition and other religious institutes, male and female, followed in their footsteps.

I do not think it is realistic to talk about the nature of religious life without some examination of the way it has existed in the Church and without regard to the motives and intentions of the founders of its various forms. Surely, if they were gifted by the Holy Spirit he would have helped them to understand the gospel. The theology of religious vows is not based on isolated texts but 'on the words and example of the Lord' (*L.G.,* n. 43). 'Religious should carefully consider that through them, to believers and non-believers alike, the Church truly wishes to give an increasingly clearer revelation of Christ. Through them Christ should be shown contemplating on the mountain, announcing God's kingdom to the multitude, healing the sick, turning sinners to wholesome fruit, blessing children, doing good to all, and always obeying the will of the Father who sent him' (*ibid.,* n. 46).

Reflecting on the history of religious life it is manifestly clear that religious, living in accordance with the spirit of their various founders, have done this. Religious obedience to the founder of a religious institute is much more than a personal response to the inspiration which one may, occasionally, be privileged to receive from charismatic personalities. It means 'to follow Christ virginal and poor (cf. Mat. 8 :20; Luke 9 :58), who, by his obedience even to death on the cross (cf. Phil. 2 :8), redeemed and sanctified mankind' (*L.G.*, n. 1). The element of renunciation and self-emptying so that one may be filled with the charity of Christ is surely a predominant theme in the theology of the vows of religion. With due respect to the authority of a scripture scholar I suggest that this is a theme which has 'genuine roots in the New Testament' and that the history of religious life shows that it has borne fruit in abundance (*supra*, p. 67).

The statement that 'a genuine religious community will certainly contribute something to its members but it contributes nothing that they cannot receive from other sources' (*supra*, p. 5) is true only in the sense that the elements which are combined together in the religious life can be found scattered throughout the life of the Church. But Father Murphy-O'Connor cannot seriously mean that the combination of such elements as daily Mass, Divine Office, religious observances, vows of poverty, chastity and obedience, formation in spirituality, apostolic activity, common life, are easily found in combination outside of the religious life. Perhaps what he means is that the combination of these elements contributes nothing towards the growth in the perfection of charity. If that is what he means he is contradicting the whole tradition of the Church on an issue which belongs to the essential nature of the Church, namely, the life of holiness. It is inconceivable that the Holy Spirit to whom is attributed the work of sanctification and from whom religious founders have received their own specific charisms would have allowed so serious a misconception to continue for so long in the Church.

Reflecting on the high ideals which our founders have formulated some of us must feel embarrassed when we contrast them with the practical realities of our daily lives. Renewal is a troublesome word. By way of consolation may I conclude with a quotation from a worthy son of St Dominic :

These are the ideals. And the realities? There have been many failures. Only the religious know how a form of life that was constructed to express generous love may at times narrow and harden. Yet it is something to have aimed high, to have set out climbing, to have dared the adventure of flight across a wild waste of waters. Is it *always* ignoble to have failed? A vain search for the Pole, a fruitless crossing of the Atlantic, may yet be heroic. Shall less be allowed to such as have fared

forth to God?
>   Their greatness, not their littleness,
>   Concerns mankind.
>   (Bede Jarrett, o.p., *The Religious Life,* London, 1939)

A reply to Father Peel's criticisms

Values and structures

JEROME MURPHY-O'CONNOR, O.P.

*The scriptures not the only guide, but they are
normative. ... Values before structures ... unity
rather uniformity.*

The question posed by Father Peel's title is a fundamental one,
because it involves the whole problem of the role, of sacred scripture
in the renewal of religious life. In my series of articles I deliberately abstracted from an examination of the tradition of religious
life in the Church, not because I deny its importance, but because
its tremendous variety necessarily makes any investigation superficial, and I hoped that religious would instinctively confront their
own understanding of religious life (formed by that tradition) with
the teaching of the New Testament. Father Peel's reaction indicates that this idea did not come across with sufficient clarity, and
so I shall attempt to be more explicit.

THE PRIMACY OF SCRIPTURE

The importance of scripture for religious has been underlined on
more than one occasion by Vatican II. In *Dei Verbum* we read :

> This sacred Synod earnestly and specifically urges all the
> Christian faithful, too, *especially religious,* to learn by frequent

reading of the divine scriptures the 'excelling knowledge of Jesus Christ' (Phil. 3 :8). 'For ignorance of the scriptures is ignorance of Christ' (n. 25; my italics).

The reason for such emphasis appears clearly in *Perfectae Caritatis*:

> Since the fundamental norm of the religious life is a following of Christ as proposed by the gospel, such is to be regarded by all communities as their supreme law (n. 2).

In the New Testament Christ is presented not only as God's invitation to men, but as the perfect model of man's response to God, and the understanding of Christ displayed in the New Testament has always been recognized by the Church as normative. In terming this understanding as 'the supreme law' of religious life the Council gives the New Testament a critical function with regard to the specific historical manifestations of religious life. In other words, customs and traditions must be evaluated in the light of the New Testament, and by mentioning 'wholesome traditions' (*Perfectae Caritatis*, n. 2) the Council implicitly recognizes that some traditions may have grown up which are not wholesome (cf. also *Perfectae Caritatis*, n. 3).

As a concrete example of what such critical evaluation implies let us turn to the primitive Dominican constitutions which Father Peel quotes with such approval. In the light of the Council documents no religious institute can escape the obligation of submitting its own constitutions to the same type of scrutiny.

CRITICISM OF CONSTITUTIONS

By its position at the very beginning the Dominican constitutions recognize that the fundamental directive covering religious life is that we have 'one heart and one mind in the Lord'. This is in perfect accord with the basic thrust of the New Testament which equates 'putting on Christ' (Gal. 3 :27) with 'putting on love which binds everything together in perfect harmony' (Col. 3 :14). This initial directive is drawn from the *Rule of St Augustine* which begins : 'The first thing for which you are gathered together is that you should dwell in harmony (*unanimes*) in the house, and have one mind and one heart in God.' This point is returned to a little later, 'Let all live together having one heart and one soul.'

Judged in the light of the New Testament the relationship of the Dominican constitutions to the rule of St Augustine is seen to manifest both authentic and inauthentic development. By emphasizing that our external conduct indicates the unity present in our hearts the Dominican constitutions take an authentic step forward, because one of the functions of the Christian community according to St Paul is to 'hold forth the word of life' (Phil. 2(16). Here we find in embryonic form the existential witness of community life with which my articles were concerned. An exhaustive examination is not possible here, but it is worth while remarking that the same existential dimension appears in a number of other contexts. For example, 'Among the principal observances of the Order which foster the contemplation of divine truth, the personal sanctification of the brethren, and *the edification of the faithful,* the first place is held by the solemn recitation of the divine office by which the Church offers worship to its divine spouse.' Shared prayer is one way in which the religious community becomes visible and has an existential impact on those it is destined to serve.

In a number of other respects, however, the primitive Dominican constitutions take a step backwards with respect to the rule of St Augustine. Where the latter speaks of 'unanimity' in the sense of having 'one mind and one heart', the constitutions allude to 'unity'. So far so good, but the constitutions then go on to equate 'unity' with 'uniformity', since uniformity is presented as the external expression of unity. Now, no one will deny that a certain degree of uniformity is essential to genuine unity. If a group is to be inspired by an effective unity of purpose there must be some uniformity of view regarding both means and end. The Dominican constitutions, however, imply that *absolute uniformity* is the only adequate expression of unity. Otherwise one cannot explain the importance given to putting in writing 'the things we are obliged to do'.

Secondly, the Dominican constitutions insist on the importance of written legislation 'lest through neglect of the smallest detail we gradually *fall away*'. It is precisely such formulations as this which give the lie to Father Peel's assertion that the traditional phrase 'state of perfection' when applied to the religious life meant merely 'school of perfection'. The idea of 'falling away' unambiguously implies that perfection has already been attained. One can only fall from the top of the mountain when one has in fact stood there. This view becomes understandable only on the assumption that the legislation of the order embodied the perfection demanded of the religious, and that this assumption did in fact dominate is clearly demonstrated by Father Peel's evocation of the frequent recurrence of the phrase 'faithful to choir and refectory' in Dominican hagiography. Total observance of the rule and constitutions was the criterion of sanctity. Inevitably, therefore, superiors insisted on perfect obedience which manifested itself externally as absolute uniformity. Singularity in dress or behaviour was not simply viewed as a divisive element, as Father Peel asserts, it was seen as a form of deviationism which indicated how far the individual was from the standard of perfection which was the key to eternal life. Thus understood, the religious life was the antithesis of a 'school of perfection'. It was a 'state of perfection', and woe betide him who slipped.

When judged in the light of the New Testament, this view of religious life stands utterly condemned. Not only is it totally at variance with the teaching of Jesus, particularly in the parables of growth, but it contradicts Paul's doctrine of the progressive development of the Christian life. Speaking of himself he says, 'I am not perfect' (Phil. 3 :12), and his epistles abound in exhortations to growth (cf. G. Montague, s.m., *Growth in Christ. A Study of St Paul's Theology of Progress*, Kirkwood-Fribourg, 1961), culminating in the assertion that it is only at the end of time that we shall attain 'to the unity of faith and of the knowledge of the Son of God, to mature manhood, to the measure of the stature of the fullness of Christ' (Eph. 4 :13). Moreover, the understanding of religious life as a 'state of perfection' involves a concept of the role of law which is totally unchristian. In fact, it is precisely the understanding of law explicitly condemned by St Paul as the greatest obstacle to the true comprehension of Christ as God's gift and demand (cf. my article on 'Moral Discernment' in DOCTRINE AND LIFE, March 1971, pp. 127-34). Hence, it is not at all surprising that Vatican II should have implicitly rejected this view of religious life. To anyone familiar with Roman procedures the fact that the Council documents nowhere use the terminology 'state of perfection' is highly significant. The omission is not accidental. In the light of the New Testament the Church itself has adopted a critical stance with regard to one of the most dominant elements in religious life as it has actually existed in the Church. In this the Church is only being faithful to her own understanding of the role of scripture. It may not be sufficient, but it is a priceless instrument of renewal from whose use no one is permitted to dispense himself.

EMOTIONAL ATTACHMENT TO THE PAST

However, the 'state of perfection' mentality with its concern for uniformity is so deeply rooted in the hearts of those who have spent most of their religious lives under its aegis that it will not be easily eradicated. There are many who, out of obedience to the Church, have abandoned the concept of 'state of perfection', but in most cases the abandonment is purely intellectual. Emotionally they are bound to the practical consequences of the very idea they reject. Lack of uniformity is seen as destructive of unity. Personal initiative appears 'to be oddly at variance with the self-emptying which is a condition of charity and hence of community'. The roots of this emotional attachment are manifold.

In the first place, it is the easy way out. This may seem paradoxical to those who see a desire for necessary change as a move towards laxity. They feel that they carry the heavy burden of observance, and contend that the others just don't care. That they carry a.burden no one can deny, but is it the burden that Christ wants us to carry? Anyone who takes the New Testament seriously must answer in the negative. The position of such religious is analogous to that of the rich young man in the gospels. Jesus loved him because he manfully shouldered the heavy burden of responsibility that his wealth imposed upon him. Yet he refused the release that Jesus offered him because he was perceptive enough to recognize that that would impose a still greater burden. In the same way many Jews, those who 'labour and are heavy burdened' (Mat. 11 :28) refused the liberation from the law that Jesus offered. The reason for such attachment becomes apparent only in the letters of Paul who clearly saw that attachment to the law with its multitudinous obligations was a facet of sinful man's flight from responsibility. When law (in our context the rule and constitutions) is given too great importance (e.g. by being made the criterion of perfection) human responsibility is sacrificed. The law makes all the decisions to which man merely submits, and thereby loses his freedom. St Thomas Aquinas is categorical on this point, 'A man who acts of his own accord, acts freely, but one who is impelled by another is not free. He who avoids evil, not because it is evil, but because a precept of the Lord forbids it, is not free. On the other hand, he who avoids evil because it is evil is free' (Commentary on 2 Cor. 3 :17). If man is to mature in response to the demand of God in Christ he must make a personal decision as to what God is calling him to do in any given situation. This is not easy. In fact it is intolerably difficult because the components of any situation are complex. Inevitably there are those who unconsciously take the easy way out by investing the letter of rule and constitutions with complete authority.

Secondly, sinful man has a powerful drive towards peace and security. The selfish do not like to be disturbed. When pressed to consider the needs of the present they look nostalgically to the past when there was 'a certain lack of haste; a leisurely movement; a contemplative spirit; an atmosphere of calm objectivity'. The lazy accept only the demands of routine. The routine of religious is established by rule and constitutions. Hence, it is in the interest of the egocentric to emphasize the importance of observance, because it serves to mask his weakness. Concern for regularity can easily lend an air of respectability to the attitude of those who simply don't want to be bothered by anything that might disturb their style of life.

Thirdly, observances are felt to be educative. Thus, for example, the primitive Dominican constitutions, '. . . in order that the uniformity maintained in our external conduct may *foster* and indicate the unity which should be present interiorly in our hearts'. This root of the emotional attachment to rules and constitutions as having the last word differs from the two previously discussed in that it does not involve a subtle form of self-deception. It springs from a genuine concern for progress of younger members of the community. Yet, there is room for misunderstandings. Many share the assumption of the Dominican constitutions that commitment to a value can be achieved by compulsory repetition, and it is in this perspective that they see the educative function of their rule. This view is open to the simple but utterly destructive objection that in practice it does not work. Parents fall into this error just as frequently as religious. They believe that by bringing or sending a child regularly to Mass or confession they are forming a habit which will persist throughout his life. A conversation with anyone involved in pastoral work among people in their twenties or late teens will soon dispel such criminal naïvete. Most of the students who enter the medical faculty at UCD have ceased to go to Mass by the time they reach their fourth year, and such examples could easily be multiplied.

I find the same lack of realism implied in Father Peel's statement that 'Father Murphy-O'Connor cannot seriously mean that the combination of such elements as daily Mass, divine office, religious observaces, vows of poverty, chastity and obedience, formation in spirituality, apostolic activity, common life, are easily found in combination outside of religious life. Perhaps what he means is that the combination of these elements contributes nothing towards the growth in the perfection of charity.' I certainly don't deny that religious life embodies this unique combination of elements. My concern, however, is with the domain that Father Peel conveniently ignores, namely, the *effectiveness* of the combination.

The results could be judged by the number of saints that a given congregation has produced, and here the statistics are far from impressive. The Dominicans whose sanctity has been officially recognized by the Church constitute a small fraction of 1 per cent of the total membership of the order since its inception. My use of statistics in this context will annoy many, but if people seriously think of religious life as a 'school of perfection' they must accept that the criteria applicable to other schools also apply to it. There are two ways of avoiding the implications of the criterion of effectiveness. The most despicable is that proposed by Father Bede Jarrett and quoted by Father Peel, namely, the romanticization of failure. A heroic failure is still a failure, and unfortunately most failures are far from heroic. To dare 'the adventure of flight across a wild waste of waters' in an inadequate machine is evidence both of courage – and of stupidity. The 'greatness' of religious is what in fact concerns mankind. How, then, can we dare to glorify the 'littleness' that is so evident? The other evasive tactic is to speak of the multitude of 'hidden souls' whose sanctity is never recognized by the Church. The use of the adjective 'hidden' is already indicative of an attempt to take the matter out of the realm where verification is possible, and so betrays an immature fear of facing reality.

If we lower our sights a little we can judge the traditional understanding of religious life by the number of really good Christians it produces. No statistics are possible here, but each one has his own experience to guide him. Given the number of religious that each of us knows, can we honestly say that the majority are worthy of respect, admiration, and imitation? Unless we can answer in the affirmative – and I personally cannot – we have to admit that religious life is producing a greater number of failures than of successes. This is the principal reason why the Council found it necessary to call for the renewal of religious life.

STRUCTURES ARE NOT VALUES

As the first step towards such renewal the Council deliberately abandoned the idea of religious life as a 'state of perfection', and so implicitly expressed a negative judgement on the idea that perfection can be achieved by enforced repetition of a pattern of behaviour considered appropriate to that state. Religious life can only be a 'school of perfection' in the real sense when rules and constitutions are seen as guidelines and not as matters of binding obligation. They are pointers to values which have always rightly been held in honour. It is in this perspective that the study of the history of religious life is worthwhile. Father Peel, however, does everyone a disservice by failing to draw a clear distinction between the perennial values of religious life and the historically contingent structures in which these values have been expressed. The essential continuity of religious life is to be found on the level of the values which are those of the New Testament. Structures have been, and will continue to be, transitory.

Let us take the example of prayer. Prayer is an indispensable element in the Christian life, and when Christians live together in community it is natural and inevitable that they should pray together. Hence, community prayer has always been a part of religious life in all the various forms this latter has taken. Father Peel cannot 'safely generalize' and say that in the post-Reformation period 'personal prayer in silence replaces the choral chanting of the divine office'. This is not merely misleading. It is false. The Jesuits had their litanies, and all the other congregations funded in this period had similar communal prayers. Such sharing of prayer on the part of those who live together is the perennial Christian value (e.g. Mat. 18 : 19-20). Choral recitation of the office, litanies, the rosary, etc., are structures in which this value found expression.

The main thrust of religious formation should be the inculcation of the value. It should be directed towards *convincing* the members that praying together is important for the building of true community. The role of authority is to *inspire* individuals with the desire of praying together. A chapter neglects its real responsibility if it contents itself with legislating for a particular structure. Naturally this is much easier than finding ways and means to bring the truth home to people in a vital way, but is the easier path the Christian way, the way of the cross? To legislate for structures risks making them permanent, but this is a quality that belongs only to values. A unique value can be expressed in a variety of ways. Shared spontaneous prayer is just as much an authentic expression of the value of community prayer as the choral recitation of the office; so is the singing of meaningful hymns.

Religious life becomes a true 'school of perfection' when, for example, local communities are permitted to determine for themselves the concrete structure in which the value of shared prayer is to be embodied. By being forced to make its own decision a community enjoys the freedom without which genuine maturity is impossible, and assumes the burden of responsibility without which maturity remains only an ideal. What the community decides will be a clear indication of its estimate of the importance of the value. A community that agrees to pray together three times a day obviously places a higher values on shared prayer than a community that meets only once a day. The work done by the community is not a factor here, because we are all capable of making sacrifices for the things we believe to be really important. If practice gives the lie to theory authority is called upon to play its role which is to inculcate a more intense appreciation of the value – and to let the community try again. Mistakes may be made. Structures thought to be attractive may reveal unforseen difficulties in practice. Such experiences, however, are the very stuff of maturity. The important thing is to discover a structure in which the value becomes real here and now. Not all communities within the same congregation may adopt the same structure, because aptitudes and tastes differ. This can be objected to only if uniformity is seen as a value, and if it is seen as a value it means that it is identified with unity. Unity, however, is a matter of the heart, not of the limbs or the voice.

THE FOUNDER'S PRAYER STRUCTURE

Father Peel rightly points out that I did not give sufficient attention to the intention of the founder, but I hope that my reply to Father Fox has done something to make up for this deficiency. Here, however, we touch another aspect of the problem, because a particular form of prayer is always laid down in the primitive rule and constitutions of different congregations. Is a congregation obligated to maintain this structure? This question can be answered only when a number of other questions have been answered first.

Were a number of other options open to the founder? If so, why did he or she choose this particular one? To what extent was he or she committed to the structure rather than to the value it expressed? I cannot hope to answer these questions for all congregations, but I hope that the position of St Dominic will be sufficiently typical to be useful.

There is not the slightest hint that he ever gave thought to the form of community prayer that his brethren should adopt. Before founding the order he had been a canon regular of Osma where he became accustomed to the choral recitation of the divine office, and at that time no other options were available. Hence, when he began to gather disciples around him he simply gave them the structure of community prayer that he knew. We know nothing of his possible attitude towards other forms of prayer-sharing. Certainly we cannot say that he condemned them because he knew only one as appropriate (in his time) for a community of clerics. Consequently, it cannot be maintained that the Dominican order is bound to the choral recitation of the divine office in virtue of the charism of its founder.

Those who contest this conclusion can do so only in virtue of an unjustifiably selective view of St Dominic's charism. One value that was certainly part of St Dominic's charism as a founder was the preaching of the word of God. In his time, however, that value could be expressed in only one way, namely, verbal proclamation, and we know from his contemporaries how much he insisted on this particular structure. We have here a precise parallel to his stress on the importance of the divine office. Yet today we know that this value can be preserved in a number of different ways. There are Dominicans who exercise a fertile apostolate of the pen, or who teach in a secondary classroom, and who rarely, if ever, preach a sermon orally. Has the order been unfaithful to its original inspiration in permitting this? Obviously not, because the value in question, though limited in the understanding of the founder to a particular structure, is not so limited in and of itself. The same must be true of the value of community prayer.

WHY CHANGE A STRUCTURE?

Since, as we have seen, a variety of structures can adequately express a single value, it is wrong to think of a structure as either good or bad in itself. It is at once more precise and more useful to classify structures as either helpful or harmful, because a structure is essentially an intermediary. One can think of a value without giving it any particular expression, but a structure makes a value part of daily life. It mediates the value by giving it a social context into which individuals can enter. For example, the value of shared community prayer can be realized only when a number of individuals are called together and a pattern of prayer laid before them. Hence, it is never sufficient to say that a particular structure is an authentic or valid expression of the value, because this judgement relates a structure in only one direction (i.e. towards the value) whereas its very nature demands that it embrace both poles (i.e. the value and the people involved). In consequence, it is inadequate and dishonest to focus exclusively on the traditional character of a structure, because this is nothing more than a guarantee of its authentic relationship to a value. It does not decide the question of whether it is helpful or harmful.

A structure is helpful if it positively encourages a deeper and more personal appreciation of the value expressed. A structure is harmful if it creates a block to commitment to the value. In both these definitions it will be noticed that the present tense is used. It is the most natural and instinctive formulation, and clearly indicates that the judgement on a structure concerns its helpfulness or harmfulness *in the present*. That the same structure should have proved helpful or harmful in the past is irrelevant. Aristotle has pointed out that a true opinion becomes false when the fact alters. Hence, the effectiveness of structures is modified as people change, and people change not only in the course of history, but in the course of their own lifetime. The blaring rhythms of a folk Mass constitute an appropriate structure of shared prayer for teenagers, but not for people in their sixties. That there is also a change from one generation to another is formally recognized by *Perfectae Caritatis*, 'The manner of living, praying, and working should be suitably adapted to the physical and psychological conditions of today's religious, and also ... to the requirements of a given culture' (n. 3).

The mention of 'psychological conditions' gives wide latitude in judging the effectiveness of a structure. It is sufficient reason to change a structure if the majority in a local community feel, however inarticulately, that a change is necessary. One concrete test that can be applied to an existent structure is this : is it observed with resignation or with enthusiasm? do people go eagerly or reluctantly? Resignation and reluctance are indications that the individual's attention is more likely to be concentrated on his or her subjective state rather than on the value. Those in authority cannot in conscience consider themselves as fostering a school of perfection if they insist on maintaining a structure which breeds resentment rather than appreciation. They cannot in honesty claim that they are safeguarding a value if their action only succeeds in turning people against that value as it is concretely expressed.

By alluding to 'the requirements of a given culture' the above text from *Perfectae Caritatis* alerts us to a further dimension of the problem. A religious community does not exist for itself. It is a school of perfection in order that the members may learn to give, not only to each other, but also to those outside, both individually and corporately. The structures of community life are a necessary part of the corporate witness which is the community's *raison d'être*. They are the visible embodiment of the values it professes. Hence, structures must be helpful not only to those in community but also to those whom it professes to serve. The majority in a given community may be perfectly content to sing the divine office in Latin, but they have to ask themselves if this is the best way to communicate the value of shared prayer to a generation that knows no Latin. Or a community may schedule its shared prayer for times which make it impossible for interested non-members to participate. It is in domains such as these that the idea of sacrifice becomes relevant, not in the giving up of a structure that is venerated simply because it is traditional.

A structure, therefore, is designed to bring a value within the reach of those outside and inside the community. In order that it should do so effectively the community should be prepared to be flexible. Since there is no necessary relationship between a value and any particular structure that authentically represents it there is no reason for a community to bind itself permanently to one structure, even when this has been freely chosen. The mood of a community changes, and if the community is honest this should be reflected in its prayer. Some prayer-structures are more apt to the expression of joy while others harmonize more perfectly with recollection or sorrow. The quality of community is very accurately mirrored in the facility with which a community switches to the mode it feels to be appropriate. There will be no difficulty if the community is truly of 'one heart and soul'. Objections will be raised in the name of tradition, regularity, and uniformity by those more concerned to find a respectable disguise for their laziness and selfishness than to permit their fellow-members to enjoy the freedom of the children of God and to worship their Father in spirit and in truth.

For the sake of clarity this article has concentrated on but one example, that of community prayer, to illustrate the relationship between values and structures. The history of religious life highlights many other values, poverty, chastity, obedience, silence, work, etc. The evolution in their structures of expression that Father Peel has sketched does not end for any given congregation at the moment of its foundation. Vatican II obliges each community to a critical evaluation of its structures, and scripture remains a perennial call for the rectification of our hierarchy of values.

What is Religious Life?

*I regret having to make these criticisms of Fr
Murphy-O'Connor's treatise, which in fact is a
very interesting work. His aim was the praiseworthy one of giving a fresh presentation of the
religious life, not just repeating things that had
been said thousands of times. It is evident that he
has thought deeply about the religious life today
and he has endeavoured to show its relevance in
the modern world. I hope the reader of these lines
will also read Fr Murphy-O'Connor's treatise.*

In the first of his articles on religious life, Fr Jerome Murphy
O'Connor, o.p., states the basis on which his whole treatise rests :
'What is most distinctive about the religious life is not the acceptance of the "evangelical counsels" as a way of life, but the fact
that religious attempt to live this acceptance *in community*. Historically the distinctive charatceristic of a religious is participation
in common life.'

This certainly is a revolutionary concept of the religious life.
One would imagine that the historical evidence, so far from
supporting it, points in the opposite direction. One thinks immediately of the early anchorites and hermits, who represent the
original form of the religious life. The very word 'monk' (in
Grek, *monachos*) literally means a solitary.

Fr Murphy-O'Connor, however, has an answer. Referring to the
Desert Fathers, he says that though they strove to live the gospel in
all its radicality, 'we do not call them "religious" in the strict
sense'.

But, on the contrary, it would seem that the term 'religious' applies, and has always been applied, in its strictest and fullest sense, to men like St Anthony of Egypt and his followers. Fr Timothy Schaefer, o.f.m.cap., in his classical work, *De Religiosis* (3rd ed., Rome 1940, n. 35) says : 'In the nature of things common life is not required for the religious state. The hermits and anchorites were, in the true sense, religious'.

It is true that in the present legislation of the Latin Church the eremitical life does not find any formal recognition. Nevertheless, even today some of our monastic orders, like the Carthusians and the Camaldolese, are predominantly eremitical, with only a bare minimum of community life. For that matter, the 'solitude' of the ancient Egyptian hermits was only relative : they lived in colonies around a master.

THE FRANCISCAN TRADITION

In Franciscan spirituality there has always been a strong tendency towards the contemplative life, a tendency that has often expressed itself in a desire for solitude. It began with St Francis himself, who frequently retired for long periods to remote places in order to be alone with God.

The early Franciscan dwellings were called 'places', but also 'hermitages' and 'retreats'. In later centuries special provision was made for those friars who felt a call to the contemplative life and wished to live in 'houses of recollection'. (Cuthbert, *Capuchins*, I, p. 30; Capuchin Constitutions, 1968, revision, n. 42.)

The origin of the Capuchin Order was associated with a revival of the eremitical and contemplative life. The Bull of Pope Clement VII, *Religionis Zelus,* dated 3 July 1528, which gave canonical status to the Capuchin reform, described the new fraternity as 'Friars Minor of the Eremitical Life'. It was assumed as a first principle that only a few friars should dwell in any one place, and that the place would be, by preference, remote, yet within easy reach of towns and villages.

There does not seem to be any foundation for the assertion that living in community is the characteristic, or basic, element of the religious life.

THE TEACHING OF VATICAN II

Father Murphy-O'Connor's concept of the religious life brings him into conflict not only with history and tradition, but also with the express teaching of the Second Vatican Council. The justification of the religious life lies, he says, in its *witness potential* (p. 11), in the fact that, even better than a family, a religious community can bear witness to true christian values. Hence he concludes : 'The degree of privacy that, in the past, was accepted as natural can no longer be maintained ... a community cannot isolate itself in restricted areas to which only members have access'. (p. 52)

But Vatican II says precisely the opposite. Speaking of the *solitude* and *silence* of contemplative communities the Council says : 'This withdrawal from the world ... should be preserved with the utmost care' (*Decree on Renewal of Religious Life*, n. 7).

THE TEACHING OF SAINT THOMAS

However important the witness value of the religious life may be, its esential value, as understood in christian tradition, goes far deeper.

The traditional notion of the religious state has never been better expounded than by Fr Murphy-O'Connor's illustrious confrère, St Thomas Aquinas (who died in 1274), to whom Fr Murphy-O'Connor never once refers. One of the weaknesses of his thesis is that it gives no satisfactory explanation of why religious are called 'religious'. St Thomas, following St Augustine, derives the word 'religion' from the latin *religare*, which means 'to bind'. Religion, therefore, is the virtue that binds man to his Creator. By the three vows religious are bound to God in a special way, and therefore in a special way they are called 'religious'.

The supreme act of religion is sacrifice, in which man offers something to God in token of homage. In religious profession a person offers to God, not something distinct from himself, but his very self. The religious self-oblation has traditionally been called a sacrifice or even a holocaust. Therefore in a special sense the term 'religious' applies to those who make this self-offering. (St Thomas, *De Perfectione Vitae*, c. XI; *Summa Theologica*, II-II, 186, 1).

If this language seems exaggerated we should remember that it is used by St Paul in reference to Christians in general : 'My brothers, I implore you by God's mercy to offer your very selves to him : a living sacrifice, dedicated and fit for his acceptance'.

(Rom., 12 :1). At each Mass all the participants are expected to renew this self-oblation in union with Christ's own offering of himself.

Just as the religious consecration is only a carrying further of the consecration of each Christian at baptism (as Vatican II states), so the self-oblation that takes place at religious profession does not differ essentially from what is expected of each Christian. The difference lies in the radical means chosen, namely the three vows.

THE ROLE OF THE VOWS

Father Murphy-O'Connor does not satisfactorily explain the function of the three vows in the religious life, or why there should be three vows at all, or just three vows, no more, no fewer.

There is no evidence that in the early religious institutes there was an explicit taking of the three vows as we know them, but there was a public commitment to a life according to the three evangelical counsels.

The gospels contain a great many counsels, but in the course of time three of them were singled out as having a certain pre-eminence. St Thomas explains this pre-eminence by the fact that each of the counsels covers a distinct sphere of human life, and between them they all cover human life in its entirety. Therefore, there could not be a fourth counsel of the same order as the existing three : there would be no room for it.

According to St Thomas the chief of the three vows is that of obedience, because by this vow a person gives to God something of greater value than what he gives by the other two : his own will, that independence of will which a person could lawfully enjoy in any other walk of life.

It is well known that St Francis reckoned poverty (which St Thomas placed last) as the chief of the evangelical counsels. There is, however, no real opposition between the view of St Francis and that of St Thomas. For Francis poverty was a very comprehensive virtue. Whenever he thought of poverty he thought of Christ, and the life of voluntary poverty for him meant a life in imitation of the poor Christ, and, therefore, in a sense, included all the christian virtues, even obedience. He saw religious obedience as a way of practising poverty. He said : 'Whoever retains *the purse of self-will* has not yet left all things for God'.

The donation of one's entire life to God is achieved most effectively by means of a vow. St Thomas explains : a person's life consists of a succession of acts spread over time. By means of a vow a person is enabled, as it were, to lay hold of them all in one act and thus offer them all together to God.

Many generations of religious have been sustained in their lives of self-dedication by the belief that even the most humble actions, when done out of obedience, were for that reason all the more pleasing to God. St Thomas says : 'Supposing that a religious, in accordance with the requirements of his state, does some good work that is small in itself, the work nevertheless receives *a great intensity* by its relation to that first binding act by which he totally dedicated himself to God'. 'A work done in fullfilment of a vow is more meritorious than if it were done without a vow, because the fulfilling of a vow is an act of religion.' (II-II, 188, 6).

THE VOWS DEVALUED

A totally different concept of the religious life is presented by Fr Murphy-O'Connor. In reference to the vow of obedience he says : 'Any impression that authority is deciding for the religious must be scrupulously avoided. The role of authority is to present material for a decision that the member of a community will take for himself.' (p. 29)

Whatever one may think of this notion of 'authority', one thing is certain : the adoption of it in practice would be, not an updating of the religious life, but changing it into something else.

From the beginnings of monasticism down to Vatican II (inclusive) religious obedience, like obedience in any other sphere of life, has meant acting on decisions made by another. Religious obedience, unlike other forms of obedience, is freely chosen and involves one's entire life. It means the sacrifice of a person's natural freedom to manage his own life.

It is the teaching of St Paul that persons invested with any form of lawful authority act in the place of God, and that he who resists authority resists God. (Romans, 13 :2). Today there is a widespread resentment against all authority, and hence it is not surprising that people do not take kindly to religious authority.

Attention is called to abuses of authority, both ecclesiastical and civil. Seven and a half centuries ago St Francis of Assisi was well aware that authority can be abused. In his Rule he made elaborate provision against such abuse, and by limiting the terms of office ensured that power would not corrupt. Yet in his Testament, though founder of his Order, he declared : 'I am resolved to obey the Minister General and that guardian whom it shall please him to set over me; and I shall so place myself in his hands that I shall be able neither to do anything nor to go anywhere except by obedience.'

If authority can be abused, so can liberty. In fact man's chief trouble ever since the time of Adam has been his misuse of freedom. If we want to lay stress on the witness value of the religious life today, might we not see it as a providential way of bearing witness against the excesses of the modern cult of freedom?

New also is Fr Murphy-O'Connor's idea of religious poverty : 'The essence of the vow of poverty is sharing' (p. 54). He sees the model of the religious life in the primitive christian community in Jerusalem. Why did those Christians g~t rid of their property? In order to 'raise the standard of living of needy members' (p. 43). St Thomas, on the contrary, sees the vow of poverty as primarily a means of self-donation to God. Thus it would still have meaning in an ideal welfare state where there would be no needy members to be helped.

The value of a celibate community to the Church, according to Fr Murphy-O'Connor, is that it 'shocks' people into asking : 'What makes them different?' (p. 59).

Reducing the value of the vows to their function of witness results in an extremely *externalist* concept of the religious life. The traditional teaching is that the taking and the observing of the religious vows are good acts in themselves irrespective of whether they take place in full view of the public or not. And the dogma of the Communion of Saints means that all acts which are good in themselves, even when performed in the utmost secrecy, are beneficial to the whole Church.

What is Religious Life?
—A Reply to Father David

JEROME MURPHY-O'CONNOR, O.P.

Father David has managed to compress an amazing amount of critcism into a brief article. All the major points that I was concerned to make about religious life are systematically contradicted. If Father David is right, I am not only wrong but utterly and completely wrong. Hence, some comment on my part is obviously necessary.

RELIGIOUS AND COMMUNITY

From my point of view the most distinctive feature of Father David's article is the highly selective way in which both he and his sources use evidence. All possible abberations regarding not only religious life but also dogma and morality are to be found in the long history of the Church. It has been said that it is virtually impossible to invent a completely new heresy. Hence, the phenomena of history cannot be simply referred to because they support a given author's position, but must be judged critically. To do so demands a fixed point of reference which all accept as true. Following Vatican II which more than once stresses that Sacred Scripture is the supreme law of religious life (*Dei Verbum*, n. 25; *Perfectae Caritatis*, n. 2) I based my interpretation of religious life on the New Testament, a work whose authority is undeniably superior to that of St Thomas Aquinas, St Francis, or Father Timothy Schaefer. The contributions of such personages must be judged in the light of Scripture.

Father David quotes with approval St Thomas' definition of 'religious'. I accept that this term is derived from the latin *religare* meaning 'to bind', but I query the justification of the unproven assumption that the reference is to the 'bond' joining Creator and creature. Nowhere in either Old or New Testament is man said to be 'bound' to God, but it is clearly asserted that Christians are 'bound' to each other : 'And above all put on love which binds everything together in perfect harmony' (Col. 3 :14). One could define a religious, therefore, as one who is bound to his or her community in a special way.

Such arguments, of course, prove nothing, because etymology never provides a secure basis for meaning. The Greek work *skandalon* originally meant a 'key', but as used in the New Testament it obviously means a 'stumbling block'. What sense would it make for Paul to present Jesus Christ as 'a key to Jews and folly to gentiles' (1 Cor. 1 :22)? Whatever the original meanings of 'monk' and 'religious', their sense today is determined by usage. And today everyone knows that a monk or religious is a Christian who belongs to a particular type of community. Specifically different terminology is used to designate solitaries. My point was that if we look at the history of those Christians who have felt themselves to have received a special call from God we find that this note of 'belonging' is a consistent element, and that it always has a point of reference below God. If in certain instances this 'belonging' is attenuated, as in the case of the ancient Egyptian monks and the contemporary Carthusians and Camaldolese, this only serves to highlight the fact that the vast majority of religious throughout the centuries have belonged to specific communities. And this was my basis for stating that the distinctive characteristic of a religious is participation in common life. Hence, I started from this predominant *factual* feature of religious life.

I find it totally unrealistic to begin from an abstract view of religious life *in itself,* and in consequence have no sympathy with Father Schaefer's statement that 'In the nature of things common life is not required for the religious state'. In the nature of what things? If we substitute 'sanctity' for 'the religious state' in this statement, Father Schaefer might be able to make a case, but then he has ceased to examine the phenomenon of religious life, because sanctity is also open to those who are not religious. Or to put it another way, statements such as Father Schaefer's are more concerned with the *goal* of religious life than with the *means* to attain it. No one disputes the goal. Hence, an adequate theology of religious life must focus on the means, that is, on the traditional structures that have been considered as conducive to the attainment of that goal. But it must go beneath the structures to the values that are therein embodied. Common life is the most radical structure of the value expressed in the precept 'Love one another', and since the New Testament consistently stresses that one cannot love God without loving one's neighbour, I do not see how anyone can reasonably deny that fraternal charity is the primordial value in the order of execution. Hence, I maintain that in any discussion of religious life the primacy must be given to the structure embodying this value, namely, community.

If one takes the New Testament seriously it is only within the context of a vital community that the Christian is *empowered* by God to make the radical self-oblation on which St Paul insists, and which Father David rightly points out is a distinctive feature of religious life. However, he and many others give the impression that they believe that religious community is constituted by those who have made this self-offering, so that self-oblation comes first and community second. On the basis of the New Testament the reverse is true. Entrance into a Christian community is the God-given opportunity to really make and live this self-offering. If one were to take Father David seriously any religious community would be a community of saints, i.e. those who have effectively and totally given themselves to God. Yet we all know that this is not true. A religious community is one in which the members *strive* to make real the offering of self. And this *fact* must enter into any theology of the religious life that claims to be realistic. If it is not, it can only be on account of a lamentable confusion between the 'theoretical' and the 'real'. Things that are true in theory are not always true in fact. In theory all religious are dedicated and consecrated to the service of God and their neighbour. This does not make it a fact that all religious are in reality so dedicated. The fact is that the vast majority of religious have a long way to go before what is implied in their vows becomes a reality in their lives. Only as they bring a fervent, loving community into existence does the theoretical offering of self acquire a real dimension as the once independent individual becomes a member of the Body of Christ. Self-oblation is nothing more than acceptance that one is not the whole, that the self is nothing more than a part. How can this be true of human beings except in terms of community? The vows are a *statement* of self-oblation and community is necessary in order that this statement be made true in fact in its full radicality. The statement can be given a certain validity through service, but the full truth is exacted from us only in the continuous challenge and demand of day-to-day life in community.

THE VOWS

Before dealing with my understanding of the vows Father David puts forward his interpretation of the traditional teaching. He says that by the vow of obedience the religious gives to God 'his own will, that independence of will which a person could lawfully enjoy in any other walk of life'. It is unfortunate that Father David did not take the time to spell out precisely what he means by this. How can man give his will to God, particularly since the revelation of God demands that man make responsible decisions choosing good and avoiding evil? How can a man grow in friendship with God if he has no will whose thrust carries him forward? How can man offer himself if his will is already in the possession of another? If we take Father David literally the religious has no independence, no initiative. In consequence, he cannot choose to read one book rather than another, to pray in one way rather than another. He cannot even decide to go to the superior to ask for a permission. The absurdity is patent. Yet such conclusions are necessarily drawn if Father David's statement is taken literally.

Let us then take the statement as an unfortunate piece of theological exaggeration, and assume that it is not to be understood literally. What then can it mean? Most obviously it could mean that certain areas of human behaviour are not covered by the vow, that it does not cover such areas as scratching my head, or brushing my teeth, or reading a book, or talking to certain people at recreation. If this is what Father David means then it must be recognized that the vow of obedience *does not involve complete surrender of the will,* because I remain my own master in certain areas. Yet I doubt that Father David would accept this conclusion, any more than I do because it contradicts the radicalism of the New Testament.

To claim that the vow of obedience involves the complete loss of independence of judgement is fine rhetoric but meaningless theology. The truth of the vow is finely expressed in Father David's quotation from St Francis, 'Whoever retains the purse of self-will has not yet left all things for God'. The key word here is 'self-will'. The instinct of sinful man is to make himself the centre and object of all his willing and desiring. By the vow of obedience the religious rejects this option. The ultimate object of his willing and desiring is God through others. He vows not to be egocentric. He commits himself to be for others, and in their service he retains the responsibility of judgement which makes him an authentic human being.

What Father David says regarding acts performed under the vow is equally misleading. He gives the impression that acts are meritorious simply because they are performed under vow. The teaching of the New Testament, and the fundamental thrust of the doctrine of St Thomas, is that only charity gives an act merit in the eyes of God. Were Father David correct religious would truly be in a privileged position vis-à-vis God, because one intense act at the beginning of one's religious life would compensate for much mediocrity in what follows. Revelation is much more exigent. The Christian must ever grow in love, 'Living the truth in love, we are to grow up in every way into him who is the head, into Christ, from whom the whole Body, joined and knit together by every joint with which it is supplied, when each part is working properly, makes bodily growth and upbuilds itself in love' (Eph. 4:15-16). St Thomas' statement only makes sense in terms of revelation if he is understood to mean that the love which prompted the original commitment is also *actually* present in the acts which are its consequence. All the activity of a Christian stands under the imperative 'Love one another', and anyone concerned with the merits of his or her acts must remember the words of St Paul, 'If I have not love *I am nothing*' (1 Cor. 13:2) – whatever vows have been taken.

THE SHARING COMMUNITY

Turning now to Father David's criticisms of my interpretation of the vows, I am astonished at the casual way he deals with the vow of poverty. My interpretation is based on the New Testament, on the very text which from the very beginning of religious life has been taken as a normative description of genuine community. It is irresponsible to simply inform us that St Thomas Aquinas says something different. Does Father David mean to imply that the authority of St Thomas is superior to that of the New Testament? Unfortunately, he has once again misunderstood St Thomas. The vow of poverty can be a symbol of a *donation* of self to God only if it involves the continuing donation of material goods to others. If the vow of poverty is essentially renunciation it cannot have the symbolic value that St Thomas attributes to it. Father David's abstract vision is evident in his evocation of the ideal welfare state. No religious can afford to be concerned about the meaning of the vow of poverty in some utopia, and even if that utopia should some day exist does Father David really see no possibility of sharing?

In claiming that 'From the beginnings of monasticism down to Vatican II (inclusive) religious obedience, like obedience in any other sphere of life, has meant acting on decisions made by another' Father David does not honestly face the issue I raised. My point was that authority, and its coorelative obedience, are not univocal notions, but differ according to the type of community to which they are referred. I then went on to show that the type of authority which rules by means of binding decisions is appropriate *only* in an action-community such as the state or an army. The members of such communities (the state, the army) are bound to give obedience to such decisions. Hence, St Paul can speak as he does in Rom. 13 : 1-7.

I must digress at this point to comment on Father David's use of Rom. 13 : 2. He maintains that the meaning is that 'persons invested with *any form* of lawful authority act in the place of God' (my italics). The italicised words represent a tendentious effort to impose on St Paul a meaning that he never intended. There is a consensus among scholars of all creeds that in Rom. 13 : 1-7 St Paul is concerned with the attitude of Christians to the Roman *state,* and this interpretation is so wide-spread that ignorance is inexcusable, particularly on the part of one who uses it as the major text in his understanding of religious obedience. The teaching of Pope Pius XII on the literal sense means that if Paul is speaking formally of obedience to the state what he says *cannot* be transferred to obedience to religious authority.

The only way in which Father David can legitimately attack my understanding of the role of authority in religious life is to show that the religious community is identical with the state both in its goals and structures. Once the issue is posed in these terms the absurdity of such an attempt becomes patent. The religious community exists to provide an entirely different type of service to the individual, namely, the inspiration and opportunity to grow in love. The state is in no way concerned about the internal attitudes. If the religious community differs from the state then the function of authority in the religious community must be other than the enactment of binding ordinances.

In this perspective I would like to suggest that Father David, and others who undoubtedly share his concept of religious authority, meditate on one key passage from Paul's letters.

Addressing Philemon the Apostle says, 'Although I have authority in Christ to command you to do what is fitting, yet for love's sake I prefer to appeal to you' (v. 8). Why does Paul prefer to appeal rather than command? The answer is given in v. 14, 'I preferred to do nothing without your consent in order that your goodness might not be by compulsion but of your own free will'. What is in question here is an act of charity with regard to the runaway slave Onesimus, and Paul refuses to order Philemon to do the right thing because it would destroy the latter's free will. In order to produce a genuine act of charity Philemon had to freely choose for himself. Hence, my statement which Father David finds so objectionable, 'The role of authority is to present material for a decision that the member of the community will take for himself'. This is precisely what Paul is doing in the case under consideration. My understanding of the role of religious authority is far from new. It is in fact the oldest in the Church. Father David's understanding of religious authority is widespread, but he must face the fact that it is in opposition to the New Testament which Vatican II has insisted is the supreme law. In such matters the opinion of St Paul is of infinitely greater weight than a statement from St Francis.

EXTERNALISM

In the last analysis Father David accuses me of presenting 'an extremely *externalist* concept of the religious life'. This remark shows that he has read me with such rigid preconceptions that he has entirely failed to understand what I was trying to say. The central thrust of my presentation was to insist that the fundamental service rendered to the Church by religious was *the quality of their lives*. I maintained again and again that only a profound internal transformation gave their activity any value. My understanding of religious life is anything but externalist, and is a reaction against the externalism that pervades our theology. It is based on the concept that the religious community is a microcosm of the local Church, and on the conviction that the most profound, liberating, and inspiring image of the local Church is to be found in the New Testament.

I have no doubt that acts which are good in themselves are beneficial to the whole Church because the mysteries of God are beyond our comprehension, but presumably Father David would agree that religious exist to serve the Church. Why then does he insist on the hidden? Was the sanctity of God diminished because He revealed himself? All I ask is that we model ourselves on Christ, and show ourselves to the world as he did, in the hope that we might continue his mission of making the love of God a *reality* in the world in which we live. 'Beloved, if God so loved us, we also ought to love one another. No man has ever seen God; if we love one another, God abides in us and *his love is made real through us*' (1 John 4:11-12).

Asking the Scriptures about religious life

FRANCIS J. MOLONEY, S.D.B.

The biblical roots of Christian life, and consequently of religious life, lie not only in the call to authentic community, living, but also in the sincere following of Christ along his way of suffering and service.

A great deal of interest has been aroused recently by the discussion initiated by Fr Jerome Murphy-O'Connor in the SUPPLEMENT TO DOCTRINE AND LIFE.[1] The title of Fr Murphy-O'Connor's booklet claimed that it was the scriptural answer to the question : 'What is religious life?' However, if one is to judge from the discussion which followed in the same journal,[2] it appears that the real point at issue was not the scriptural basis of religious life, but the primacy of community living over apostolic activity. Fr Murphy-O'Connor has argued that 'The *raison d'être* of a religious community consists in the witness value of its corporate existence',[3] while Fr Fox and Fr Peel have claimed that there is something to be said for the 'action community', as each religious order or congregation has a *specific raison d'être*,[4] which is to be found in the apostolic purpose of its foundation.

The discussion is no longer concerned with the biblical roots for religious life, but centres on the importance of the charism of the founders of religious orders. Fr Peel argues from St Benedict, St Dominic and St Ignatius, while Fr Fox uses St John Bosco and his Salesians.

---

1. J. Murphy-O'Connor, 'What is Religious Life?'.

2. E. J. Fox, 'The *raison d'être* of Religious Life', SUPPLEMENT TO DOCTRINE AND LIFE, 49 (1974), pp. 3-10; H. E. Peel, 'Is Scripture Sufficient?', SUPPLEMENT TO DOCTRINE AND LIFE, 50 (1974), pp. 3-12.
3. J. Murphy-O'Connor, *art. cit.*, p. 30.
4. Cf. H. E. Peel, *art. cit.*, p. 7.

COMMUNITY IS FOR ALL

In many ways this was inevitable. Fr Murphy-O'Connor himself points out that religious life, as a distinctive form of life within the early Church, cannot be found in the New Testament.[5] Out of the New Testament, however, came the tendency for people to live together (cf. Acts and Paul). This became the distinctive mark of religious life. 'Historically, the distinctive characteristic of a religious is participation in common life.'[6] This is a historical fact which cannot be denied. If then, the mark of religious life is community living, can we turn back to the Bible and find some sort of scriptural 'basis' for this tendency? The question is almost rhetorical, as we are well aware of the community aspect of both the Old Testament people of God and the Church founded by Jesus Christ. Fr Murphy-O'Connor is correct when he points to community living as central to religious life. What he fails to spell out sufficiently, however, is that this biblical 'being community' is also, in so far as it applies to all who are addressed by the written word of God, a *universal* call.

He avoids this problem by claiming that we must be 'extremely realistic' when talking about the witness which Christian communities are called to give. Because Paul's 'local Church' bears no resemblance to our current communities of parish and diocese, he concludes that 'today only two communities are capable of furnishing the existential witness that Paul attributes to the local Church, the family and the religious community'.[7] It strikes me that this extreme realism is, ultimately, avoiding the issue. In a later discussion with Fr Peel, Fr Muphy-O'Connor insists upon the normative value of sacred scripture.[8] Has he not compromised this very principle by being 'extremely realistic' about the community witness to which *all* Christians are called?

Fr Murphy-O'Connor is correct when he writes : 'What is said in the New Testament in general can be applied strictly and liter-

5. J. Murphy-O'Connor, *art. cit.*, pp. 4-5. He quotes in support the fine article of J. M. R. Tillard, 'Le fondement évangélique de la vie religieuse', *NRT*, 91 (1969), pp. 916-955.
6. J. Murphy-O'Connor, *art. cit.*, p. 5.
7. *Ibid.*, p. 11.
8. J. Murphy-O'Connor, 'A Reply to Fr Peel's Criticisms. Values and Structures.

ally to religious life.'[9] It appears, however, that what is said there applies *only* to religious life. We should be asking ourselves why this is so. Why do we have to abandon a universal call to genuine Christian community living? This is a very serious question, and the whole of our hierarchical, diocesan and parochial system would do well to face it squarely.[10]

Fr Murphy-O'Connor bases his whole discussion on the belief that the existential witness to community living is the *raison d'être* of religious life. The existential witness to community living is a task which has been given to the whole Church. It is in their role within the Church that religious are called to their particular *form* of community witness. The fact that the Church at large and, for that matter, most communities of religious are not performing this task does not lessen the obligation.

THE CALL TO DISCIPLESHIP

Although this objection is basic, it is not the only problem which the article presents. The whole of Fr Murphy-O'Connor's discussion limps because of an inordinate focussing of attention upon the community. It would appear that this is the only scriptural answer to the question. 'What is religious life?' The polarization which has arisen from this suggestion, as evidenced by the articles of Fr Fox and Fr Peel and by the many discussions among religious who are asking themselves : 'Community *or* apostolate,' is a false one.[11] This is so because the New Testament has an equally important word to say to Christians, and thus also to religious, about discipleship. Religious communities are not *only* a witness to the value of corporate existence. They are called, like other Christians, to follow Christ. In this too they must bear witness, and this part of their lives, equally based on the scriptures, resolves the polarization between community and apostolate.

9. 'What is Religious Life?', p. 11.
10. See, for a courageous and enlightening assessment of this situation, M. Winter, *Mission or Maintenance?* (London, 1973).
11. It must be pointed out that Fr Murphy-O'Connor is well aware of this and has no intention of creating such a dilemma. As he said explicitly in the original booklet: 'I am not advocating that they should sit down and simply *be*' (p. 14). See also 'A .Reply to Fr Fox. The Charism of the Founder'.

The importance, in scripture, of the community aspect of a Christian and therefore of a religious life, has already been eloquently spelt out by Fr Murphy-O'Connor.[12] I have no desire to contradict what he has written. The whole discussion, however, remains one-legged unless we look to the equally important biblical message of discipleship.

It is beyond the scope of this article to trace the development of the idea of the Old Testament people's belonging to Yahweh, and the subsequent obligation which they had to love and serve him in their day to day lives. When the sages of Israel eventually came to write down the decalogue, they started with the words : 'I am the Lord your God' (Exod. 20:2; Deut. 5:6).

Once that fact was clear, then the various directives which Israel had to live by could follow logically. The Deuteronomist has enshrined this belief in the famous Jewish confession of faith : 'Hear, O Israel; the Lord our God is one Lord; and you shall love the Lord your God with all your heart, and with all your soul and with all your might' (Deuit. 6:4).

The Psalmist has cried out the same belief when he sang : 'Blessed is everyone who fears the Lord, who walks in his ways! You shall eat the fruit of the labour of your hands; You shall be happy, and it shall be well with you' (Ps. 128:1-2).

Israel was convinced that Yahweh had called her to be his chosen people. She knew that she belonged to him in a very special way, but she was also conscious that this privilege brought with it the burden of doing his will. The individualization of this fact is found dramatically presented in the Book of Job, and also in the lives of the prophets. The story of Jeremiah's vocation is dominated by it : 'To all to whom I send you you shall go, and whatever I command you you shall speak. Be not afraid of them, for I am with you to defend you, says Yahweh' (Jer. 1:7-8).

This knowledge and conviction that Israel and her saints belonged to God and had to be prepared to suffer the consequences may well be the background for the more personally human bond that Jesus established between himself and those whom he called to be his disciples.

12. Cf. also F. J. Moloney, 'Why Community?', SUPPLEMENT TO DOCTRINE AND LIFE, 49 (1974), pp. 19-31; 'The Communities of the Early Church', SUPPLEMENT TO DOCTRINE AND LIFE, 50 (1974), pp. 24-30.

What is said in the gospels, is, of course, sometimes the reflection of the early Church on her mission. Not all that follows comes to us directly from Jesus. This does not, however, in any way, lessen the validity of what is said.

THE DISCIPLES OF JESUS

The fundamental mark of a disciple of Jesus is that he is called by Jesus himself.[13] The initiative of God in all that pertains to the realm of grace is something that has been jealously guarded throughout the long history of Christian theology. It applies also here, in the call to follow Christ. The earliest of the gospels, Mark, spells this out very clearly : 'And Jesus said to them, "Follow me and I will make you become fishers of men" ' (Mark 1:17; cf. Mt. 4:19).

Again Mark makes this clear in the call of Levi : 'And as he passed on, he saw Levi the son of Alphaeus sitting at the tax office, and he said to him, "Follow me." And he rose and followed him' (Mark 2:14).

Not all the accounts of the calling of the disciples have this clear invitation to 'follow' Jesus, but the initiative always remains with him. In the Lucan account of the calling there is no formal invitation to 'Come, follow me', but the main feature of the passage is that Peter and Andrew obey Jesus, leaving all to follow him (cf. Luke 5:1-11). The opposite possibility is shown in Mark 5:18-20 where the Gerasene demoniac wants to follow Jesus, but is not permitted to do so.

Once called and united to him, the disciples appear to have a very special relationship with him. It is wholly personal, and it depends upon the unique nature of the person of Jesus. He was the one who called the disciple and he, in turn, gives form and content

---

13. The sketch which follows is very dependent upon K. H. Rengstorf, Article 'Mathetes' in *TDNT*, IV, pp. 444-453. See especially J. Jeremias, *New Testament Theology*, I (London, 1971), pp. 159-249. Also W. Barclay, *New Testament Words* (London, 1964), pp. 41-46; E. M. Kredel, Article 'Jünger', in J. B. Bauer, *Bibeltheologisches Worterbuch* (Graz, 1967), pp. 793-798; R. Schnackenburg, *The Moral Teaching of the New Testament* (London, 1964), pp. 42-53; 'The Call to Discipleship; S. Freyne, *The Twelve: Disciples and Apostles. A Study in the Theology of the First Three Gospels* (London, 1968).

to the relationship that must exist if the discipleship is to last. The person of Jesus, along with his powerful word, appears to have made a lasting impression upon his disciples. In Luke 5 we find the story of the calling of Peter. Simon Peter already knew Jesus, according to the Lucan account as Jesus has healed his mother-in-law in the preceeding chapter (cf. Luke 4:38-39). In telling us of Peter's call, Luke stresses the inner effect upon Peter of what Jesus does. At first Peter is full of his own knowledge and experience : 'Master, we toiled all night and took nothing!' Before the person of Jesus, however, he relents. 'But at your word I will let down the nets' (5:5). The influence of Jesus is already having effect, but this effect grows. At the miracle Peter's self-assertiveness crumbles completely before the one who confronts him. He repents and believes : 'He fell down at Jesus' knees saying, "Depart from me for I am a sinful man" ' (Luke 5:8). It is thus, as a believer, conscious of his own weakness before the person of Jesus, that Peter is made a disciple of Jesus (cf. Luke 5:10).

The disciples unconditionally accept Jesus' authority. There seems to be no murmur of dissent, with the exception of Judas, the unfaithful disciple. In some passages of the gospels the disciples are compared to slaves : 'A disciple is not above his teacher, nor a slave above his master; it is enough for the disciple to be like his teacher and the servant like his master' (Mt. 10:24-25). 'Truly, truly I say to you, a slave is not greater than his master; nor is he who is sent greater than he who sent him' (John 13:16).

In all of this,. as in most things to do with discipleship, they are but called to 'follow' Jesus, who says of himself : 'The Son of man also came, not to be served, but to serve and to give his life as a ransom for many' (Mark 10:45).

During Jesus' last days we have news of the disciples serving their master. What we find here is probably true of the whole of the time that these men spent with Jesus. On the occasion of his entry into Jerusalem he sends his disciples to find a donkey (Mark 11:1) and later he asks them to prepare the last supper (Mark 14:12-15). Jesus was obeyed because of his authority. However, they misunderstood this authority. They followed him in the hope of finding in him the political Messiah that Israel was waiting for. This belief was thwarted by the events of Good Friday. This explains the mood of the small glimpse that we are given of the period between the crucifixion and the resurrection. Deep depression marks these days. The reason for this depression is to be found in the fate which has befallen the person of Jesus. The story of the walk to Emmaus is one that puzzles biblical geographers and interpreters, but whatever one makes of the events of that walk, the fact that throughout it they spoke about Jesus and his fate (cf. Luke 24:19-24) shows how all appeared to be lost with the loss of the master.

Out of this the risen Christ reconstituted his discipleship. He again called his own to a discipleship and to a personal fellowship with him. To do this he has to restore what has been lost, so he forgives their sins and gives them authority to forgive sin (cf. John 20:22-23). The story of doubting Thomas and his restoration to faith, along with the promise made to future disciples (cf. John 20:24-29) spells this out quite clearly.

Because of the resurrection, however, something radically new happened. These disciples were called by him and linked to him in a profound way both during his ministry and after the resurrection. Under the influence' of the Spirit, they became witnesses to the revelation disclosed in the person of Jesus : 'You are witnesses of these things, and behold, I send the promise of my Father upon you' (Luke 24:48-49). The same thought is found again in Acts : 'But you shall receive power when the Holy Spirit has come upon you; and you shall be my witnesses in Jerusalem and Samaria and to the end of the earth' (Acts 1:8).

In this all-too-brief sketch of the disciples of Jesus as we find them in the gospels, I have left two aspects till last. I have done this purposely, as these are two aspects of religious life which can be missed by an over-accentuation of either a community or a personal dimension. The call to discipleship also involved :

An obligation to suffer with Jesus.
An obligation to share the work of Jesus.

THE OBLIGATION TO SUFFER WITH JESUS

Jesus called the disciples himself and consequently, these men were entirely dependent upon him. There was, therefore, nothing in their lives which could be separated from Jesus and his life. With all they had and were, they were drawn into fellowship with Jesus. But the way of Jesus led to the cross. Hence, entry into his fellowship as his disciple carried with it the obligation to suffer. It is clear in the gospels that Jesus left his disciples in no doubt that they were committing themselves to suffering if they followed him. To the twelve he says : 'Beware of men, for they will deliver you up to councils, and flog you in their synagogues and you will be dragged before governors and kings for my sake, to bear testimony before them and the Gentiles' (Mt. 10:17-18). 'If the world hates you, know that it has hated me before it hated you' (John 15:8). 'Indeed the hour is coming when whoever kills you will think he is offering service to God' (John 16:2).

This possibility came close to being a reality as Jesus was led off to his death. The group of men who were supposed to follow him along this way broke up and ran away from the dangerous situation in which they found themselves at the arrest of Jesus. Then came the change wrought by the Easter event. What happened we do not know. What resulted from it is clear from the fact that this fear was overcome and because of this, we exist today as Christians. The gospels never attempt to describe the event of Easter. Paul has likewise been unable to speak of the inner experience that changed his life. He was happy to call it 'the power of the resurrection' (cf. Phil. 3:10) which made sense of this sharing the sufferings of Christ, 'becoming like him in his death'. After, and because of the resurrection there took root among these fear-stricken men and women a joyous readiness for the suffering which Christians, as disciples of Jesus have had to endure and have constantly endured for centuries.

THE OBLIGATION TO SHARE THE WORK OF JESUS

The Lucan account of Peter's call to discipleship (Luke 5:1-11) is also a call to work with Jesus for the establishment of his kingdom : 'Do not be afraid, henceforth you will be catching men' (Luke 5:10). This is no accident. As Jesus himself never turned inwards to himself, but girded himself for service, so he instructs his disciples. His task with them during his public life is to direct their gaze and their powers to his task of establishing the kingdom of God. Because of their association with him, this task was inevitably also theirs.

Further discussion of this would lead us into the vitally important concept of 'apostle' in the New Testament, and especially in the theology of St Paul. This would be to go further than the limits which we have set upon this short paper. It is sufficient for our purposes to stay with the disciples of Jesus and to recall his instructions to them : 'You are the salt of the earth; but if salt has lost its taste, how shall its saltiness be restored?' 'You are the light of the world ... Let your light so shine before men, that they may see your good works and give glory to your Father who is in heaven' (cf. Mt. 5:13-15).

The parable of the talents (Mt. 25:14-30) with its blessing : 'Well done good and faithful servant; you have been faithful over little, I will set you over much' (Mt. 25:21, 23) and its condemnation : 'You wicked and slothful servant; You know that I reap where I have not sowed and gather where I have not winnowed ... Cast the worthless servant into the outer darkness' (Mt. 25:26, 30), must be understood as a command to the disciple to involve himself in the master's task – or to suffer the consequences.

The Johannine Jesus prays to his Father : 'As thou didst send me into the world, so I have sent them into the world' (John 17:18), and Jesus' last words to his disciples in the Gospel of St Matthew spell all this out : 'Go therefore and make disciples of all nations, baptizing them in the name of the Father and of the Son and of the Holy Spirit' (Mt. 28:19).

Thus it appears to me that the biblical roots of Christian life, and consequently of religious life, lie not *only* in the call to authentic community living, but also in the sincere following of Christ along his way of suffering and service. In saying this I do not wish to be misunderstood. The work of Fr Murphy-O'Connor, in so far as it spells out the communitarian basis of religious life, is of tremendous value. A great deal of attention should be paid to what has been said in those pages. It is equally basic, however, to the New Testament that those who are called by Christ are called to follow him. This means that both from and within their communities, they are called to fulfil a task of establishing the kingdom and of laying down their lives for the ransom of many.

THE BIBLICAL COMMUNITY

Religious life is not only 'being'. It is also 'doing'. It *must* be both. After the scene in the Fourth Gospel which tells of the washing of the disciples' feet, Jesus lays down a law which governs all Christian living : 'A new commandment I give you, that you love one another, even as I have loved you, that you also love one another. By this men will know that you are my disciples, if you have love for one another' (John 13:34-35; cf. 1 John 3:16-18, 23; 4:11). But this was not the only law which he gave. He also told those same disciples : 'For I have given you an example that you also should *do* as I have *done* to you' (John 13:16).

It appears that for the disciple, called by Christ to serve him as a religious *or* as a lay person, there can be no separation between 'being' and 'doing'.[14]

It is true that many religious and religious communities have suffered through being sacrificed to the cause of the apostolate. The solution to this problem, however, lies in the clarification of both the community and the apostolic aspects of religious life – not in the overstatement of one or the other. Fr Murphy-O'Connor has used a fine article by Fr J. M. R. Tillard on the evangelical basis of religious life.[15] I would like to conclude these pages with a paraphrase from this article which presents a balanced view of a community which must be involved in the total giving of itself to the following of Christ :

> Religious life has always found its roots in a particular grasp of the whole of the gospel message. By taking every possible means, it attempts to reach the radical commitment presented in the scriptures, firstly by that group who 'followed' Jesus and who, in doing so, became signs of the absolute value of the kingdom which was available to all who believed, and secondly in the idealistic transposition of this group, in the early Church, into the small community of Jerusalem as it is presented in Acts. This community, devoured by the fire of the Spirit, is the model of the community of the Church, and thus of a religious community.[16]

14. Again it should be noted that Fr Murphy-O'Connor has said this on several occasions during the discussion. See above, footnote 11.
15. The article is mentioned above in footnote 5.
16. Cf. Tillard, *art. cit.*, p. 953. For the detailed analysis of the material which leads to this conclusion see pp. 933-953. The final reference to the religious community is mine.

Community: The possibility of discipleship

JEROME MURPHY-O'CONNOR, O.P.

One cannot live a fully human, Christian life alone: the values of the world will swamp the endeavour. Hence the need for **Christian** *community, in which the values of the gospel are incarnate and the members mediate them to one another by their loving-care. Community makes discipleship possible.*

The 'following of Christ' is that which makes a life Christian. Hence, it must be integral to the religious life, and Father Moloney is right to emphasize the point, particularly since it occupies such a prominent place in the gospels. His article has the laudable purpose of completing my presentation so that a more-balanced view of what the New Testament is telling us can be obtained, and from an academic point of view he succeeds. However, from the point of view of a realistic theology of religious life I am afraid that his article may contribute to the perpetuation of a misunderstanding.

As presented by Father Moloney the disciples appear as a group, but this group is constituted by a series of *individual* relationships with Jesus. The disciples are together simply because each is with Jesus. This is, of course, the traditional concept of religious life. Those who have felt a call to follow Jesus more perfectly are drawn together because of their commitment to him, and so constitute a group. All too often such a group is not a community, and in many cases the root cause is that the members are much more concerned about their individual relationships to Jesus than about the relationships that should exist among themselves. The purpose of my original articles was to attempt to do something about this situation by drawing attention to parts of the New Testament that are not normally given adequate place in discussions concerning the religious life, namely, those parts which manifest the primordial importance of community. Inevitably the individual seemed to disappear into the background, and my presentation could possibly have given the impression that I was abandoning the motif of the following of Christ. This was not in any way my intention, and so I am grateful to Father Moloney for drawing attention to the point.

It is imperative for the religious both to follow Christ and to commit him or herself totally to community. Father Moloney's article, however, gives the impression that he merely juxtaposes community and following Christ. Such juxtapositioning is tantamount to setting up two poles, and in practice this will lead to polarization. In theory one could expect the religious to preserve a balance between the two, but this is artificial and carries the built-in danger of giving undue emphasis to one aspect at the expense of the other. Hence, an effort must be made to integrate the two aspects. With the exception perhaps of Matthew the evangelists do not concern themselves with this problem. However, it was one of the major preoccupations of St Paul for whom the following of Christ *was made possible* only by commitment to and life in an authentic community. This point was made in the section entitled 'The Formation Community' in my original study,[1] but Father Moloney's reaction shows that further clarification is perhaps desirable.

THE FOLLOWING OF CHRIST

In the gospels the followers of Jesus are called 'disciples'. This formula is so well-known that very often we don't even advert to the latent contradiction. Like its correspondent in Greek *mathêtês,* 'disciple' means a student. To be a disciple of X means to have studied at the feet of X with the connotation of a systematic learning process. The term, therefore, corresponds to the title 'teacher' given to Jesus. This understanding of the relationship between Jesus and his followers is from the earliest level of the gospel tradition. To all appearances he was nothing but an itinerant rabbi trailed by a group of students. However, as time went on this description was felt to be more and more inadequate. Luke realized this more keenly than any of the other evangelists, and in his gospel Jesus appears as a 'teacher' only to outsiders (e.g. Lk. 10:25;

1. SUPPLEMENT TO DOCTRINE AND LIFE, n. 45 (May-June, 1973), pp. 21-23.

22:11). The disciples address him as 'Master' (Lk. 5:5; 8:24, 45; 9:33, 49; 17:13), and it is significant that each time this title is set in close relation to the 'power' of Jesus. In other words, the disciples experienced Jesus as something more than a mere purveyor of knowledge. Paul must have had the same awareness because he never uses the words 'teacher' or 'disciple' to express the relationship between believers and Christ. What is characteristic of a 'disciple', therefore, is paradoxically not learning, but following, being with Jesus.

It is equally clear from the gospels, however, that there is 'following' and 'following'. The crowds 'follow' Jesus (Mt. 14:13) but this does not make them disciples. Something more than material association is necessary. 'If any man would come after me, let him deny himself and take up his cross and follow me' (Mt. 16:24); 'He who does not take his cross and follow me is not worthy of me' (Mt. 10:38). The function of the phrase concerning the acceptance of the cross is to underline the fact that the true disciple must model himself on Jesus. There is no authentic following of Jesus without imitation. There is no being with Jesus without assimilation of the dominant traits of his character.

THE HUMANITY OF JESUS

At this point we begin to perceive the importance of the humanity of Jesus, because it is only as man that we can imitate him. One of the major pastoral problems that St Paul had to face was how to bring his converts to a new understanding of themselves. Through baptism they had been recreated in Christ (2 Cor. 5:17). They were new men, quite distinct from the old men they had once been. In order to aid them in reducing this theory to practice he had to assist them to modify their understanding of what man could and should be. They were accustomed to taking their idea of what could be expected of man from the dominant attitudes of the society in which they lived. Hence, he had to give them another vision. He had to present them with an alternative. He had to convince them that there was a man who was radically different to the men they saw around them, a man in whom God's intent for man was manifest without any distortion. Hence, his consistent concern to present Christ as the embodiment of authentic humanity, the one man who truly was what God desired him to be. For Paul, therefore, Christ in his humanity was the standard by which men were to be judged.

Normally we are inclined to think of Christ in terms of ourselves rather than *vice versa,* and Paul's converts were no different. Paul was sympathetic with the difficulty they had in beginning to think in a different way, because he had undergone the same experience himself. To the Corinthians he writes :

> Christ died for all, that those who live might live no longer for themselves but for him who for their sake died and was raised. From now on, therefore, we know no one in a fleshly way, even though we once knew Christ in a fleshly way, we now know him so no longer (2 Cor. 5:15-16).

When Paul says that he 'once knew Christ in a fleshly way' he is referring to the period prior to his conversion when he accepted the common opinion of his contemporaries for whom Jesus was a dangerous heretical teacher rightly condemned by the Jewish authorities and executed by the Romans (Acts 9:1-2). Now, however, he recognizes that the standard by which he evaluated Christ was false, and this has convinced him that the standard by which he judged other men was also false, 'we now know *no one* in a fleshly way'. Fundamentally this means that he will no longer accept as normal and inevitable the selfishness that afflicts mankind, because 'Christ died for all, *that those who live might live no longer for themselves'.* Christians, therefore, are to live as Christ lived.

But what real significance could this type of statement have had for Paul's converts? They had never known Christ in the flesh, and the only event of his life to which Paul draws attention is his death. This forces us to look more closely at the death of Christ.

THE CREATIVITY OF LOVE

Death is an ambiguous concept because it can be validly interpreted in a number of ways. One way of viewing death is to see it as putting an end to further achievement. Once a person is dead he or she can accomplish nothing more. It is equally possible, however, to see death as in itself an achievement. A heroic death can redeem a worthless life, as in the case of the shiftless drunkard who throws himself on a grenade about to explode in a crowded street, or in the case of a death which inspires others to deeper commitment to a great cause. A third way of looking at death is to see it as focusing to exceptional clarity the achievement of a lifetime. It is in this third way that Paul views the death of Christ. His consistent emphasis that this death was 'for others' (e.g. 1 Cor. 8:11; Rom. 5:8; 14:15; Gal. 2:20) underlines his awareness that the self-giving of Christ was the dominant feature of his life.

We can take this a step further by looking at Gal. 2:20 where Paul writes, 'The life I now live in the flesh I live by faith in the Son of God who loved me and gave himself for me.' The 'and' in this sentence is explicative; 'loved me' and 'gave himself for me' mean the same thing. What then is love? The best answer is provided by John Macquarrie :

> Love in its ontological sense is letting-be. Love usually gets defined in terms of union, or the drive towards union, but such a definition is too egocentric. Love does indeed lead to community, but to aim primarily at uniting the other person to oneself, or oneself to him, is not the secret of love, and may even be destructive of genuine community. Love is letting-be, not of course in the sense of standing off from someone or something, but in the positive and active sense of enabling-to-be. When we talk of 'letting-be' we are to understand both parts of this hyphenated expression in a strong sense – 'letting' as 'empowering' and 'be' as enjoying the maximal range of being that is open to the particular being concerned. Most typically, 'letting-be' means helping a person into the full realization of his potentialities for being; and the greatest love will be costly, since it will be accomplished by the spending of one's own being (*Principles of Christian Theology*, London, 1966, 52, p. 310).

Love, in other words, is the most profound form of creativity open to man, and this of course takes us right back to the fundamental biblical definition of man as 'the image of God' (Gen. 1:26-27; cf. 1 Cor. 11:7). What is the point of similarity between man and God? The only thing we know about God from the first chapters of Genesis from which this definition is drawn is that he is *creative*. This suggests that man is truly the image of God only when he too is creative, and in this perspective it is highly significant that the only action attributed to man before the fall is generally understood as a creative act (Gen. 3:19-20). Man, therefore, only exists as God intended him to be when he loves in such a way that others are thereby enabled to become what God desires them to be.

This love Christ exhibited in its full plenitude, and as a result opened a new possibility of being to humanity. Because of him men were given an opportunity to become other than they were before. Hence, if men are to 'follow Christ' and to assume their obligation to share in his work (as Father Moloney insists), it can only be by manifesting the creative love that made Christ as man unique. Man was created by God to be the only *creative creature,* and Christ shows the type of creativity that God intended. It is a creativity directed not to technology or art but to other men. To follow Christ means to love as he did, to love in such a way that others are freed to become themselves instruments of this creative love.

THE OBSTACLES TO IMITATION

Many existentialist theologians naïvely assume that all that is necessary for imitation is the proposal of a model. They suggest that once Christ has been put forward by God as the exemplar of authentic humanity man thereby becomes capable of imitating him. The naïvete of this assumption lies in its forgetting the obvious distinction between 'knowing' and 'doing'. The mere fact that a person knows that cars can be driven does not make him capable of actually driving a car. A weak man may know the technique of lifting weights but this does not make him capable of actually lifting them. Similarly, there is a gap between knowing and admiring Christ and actually living with the creative love that inspired him. In order to follow Christ man must not only be informed, he must be *empowered.*

The reason for this is that man is subject to pressures which make it difficult, if not impossible, for him to love. Human beings do not exist in a vacuum. They are born into an already-existent society, and from the moment that they begin to learn they assimilate the attitudes prevalent in that society. This conditioning is most evident on the level of social behaviour. Certain things are done to greet a guest, a definite ritual prevails at meals. The conditioning, however, goes much deeper than that. In a competitive society children learn to be competitive. A certain mistrust of others as potential rivals is bred into their bones. In a society where certain forms of dishonesty are accepted as inevitable children grow up with a distorted sense of honesty. In a society which distinguishes between first-class and second-class citizens children absorb the idea that some men are inferior to others. These inherited attitudes are what Paul had in mind when he spoke of the power of sin, 'All men, both Jews and Greeks, are under the power of sin' (Rom. 3:9). The tyranny of social pressures constitutes a form of slavery (Rom. 6:6, 17, 20) which robs man of the freedom to be what God requires him to be.

Despite the fact that the western world has been theoretically Christian for 1500 years it would be foolish to assume that social attitudes hostile to man's authentic development (which is equivalent to following Christ) have been completely eradicated. Even the most superficial observation reveals that the world is divided into the same sort of mutually-hostile blocks that Paul observed. We may no longer distinguish between Greeks and Barbarians but the same destructive tension exists between the West and the Third World. Today women are theoretically accepted as equals, but the practice has in fact changed very little. The intense individualism that Paul fought against is still a dominant factor. Even Christians accept possessiveness as something so deeply rooted in human nature that nothing significant can be done about it. Even Christians instinctively think of God in terms of power rather than in terms of love.

THE WAY GRACE WORKS

The power needed to overcome these difficulties is nothing other than *grace*. No one will deny the necessity of grace, but most frequently there is a fatal misunderstanding as to how this grace in fact operates.

All will agree that God knows and loves each individual, but many go on to infer from this that God deals directly and immediately with each individual. There is no logical necessity in this deduction, and the dominant influence is the selfishness of sinful man. To believe that God deals directly with each individual means that I have no real responsibility for my neighbour. Anything that

I can do for him is an extra and in no way essential. The practical conclusion is that I don't need to be concerned. And this, of course, is precisely the conclusion that the selfish and lazy person unconsciously desires to arrive at. The doctrine of God's loving concern is used to give a veneer of respectability to selfishness.

The theory of direct grace is true only in so far as it emphasizes the primacy of the divine initiative. It is false to the extent that it wilfully ignores what God has told us about the way in which his grace operates. God's normal mode of acting is through the incarnational channels he inaugurated with the mission of Christ. Thus Paul can say to the Corinthians, 'we are servants *through whom* you believed' (1 Cor. 3:5). The fundamental gift of grace is not given directly but mediated through human beings. And this is the normal way in which other graces are given, as a little honest reflection on experience will show.

Those with a drinking problem are given the strength to resist by the concern of devoted friends. Those who are sad are given joy by a friend who makes an effort to take them out of themselves. The bereaved are consoled by the sympathy of a friend. Those in doubt are given wisdom through the advice of a friend genuinely sollicitous about their welfare. These examples could be mutliplied almost indefinitely, and strength, joy, consolation, and wisdom are all traditionally recognized as graces. God does not need men to communicate these graces, and in certain exceptional circumstances he can give them directly. The fundamental message of the New Testament, however, is that God has decided to *use* men as the normal channel of grace.

FREEDOM TO LOVE

What has been said in the previous section should make it obvious how dependent we are on others if we are to follow Christ. The grace that empowers us to imitate him is mediated through them. Equally we are responsible for the grace that makes it possible for them to be Christlike. The very possibility of following Christ, therefore, is conditioned by a series of reciprocal grace-filled relationships which is a very precise definition of the genuine Christian community.

It is this web of strength that constitutes the basis of Christian freedom, because it cancels out the hostile pressure of inauthentic social attitudes. The isolated individual living in the 'world' is totally at the mercy of the orientation of his environment. He is swept along because he is incapable of controlling the vast forces involved. He is no more capable of resistance than he is capable of not breathing the toxic fumes of a polluted environment. Hence, the need seen by God to create a new type of environment where man would be subject to pressures that would assist, rather than hinder, his authentic development. This new environment inaugurated by Christ is the Church whose concrete expression is the local community. Only 'in Christ' (Gal. 3:27-28) is the believer 'set free from sin' (Rom. 6:18). This does not mean that inauthentic social attitudes have been destroyed. For Paul, sin still seeks to enslave (Rom. 6:6). Hence, the supreme importance of a vital community if the individual is to have the freedom which makes the following of Christ possible, because only when he is loved in the creative way that distinguished the humanity of Christ does he become capable of exhibiting the same love which is the essence of the imitation of Christ.

DISCIPLESHIP AND COMMUNITY

Like any reciprocal relationship that between discipleship and community is a complex affair. Any one member is dependent on the community for the transmission of the grace which makes it possible for him to be another Christ. He is liberated by love, inspired by good example, and sustained by understanding and affection. Without these the power of Christ does not reach him. The evidence for this is found in the vast majority of religious communities. They contain individuals who have been members for anything up to fifty years who are mean, possessive, and destructive of other human beings. The classic response to this tragedy is to claim that there was failure to correspond with grace. It is equally possible that no really-effective grace was ever present in that situation, and this must have been the case in fact if the individual was ignored, or slighted, or not encouraged, or consoled, for all these are the incarnational mode of divine love.

If the individual is dependent on the community to be a genuine follower of Christ, it is equally true that the community is dependent on the individual. He or she must be Christ for others in the sense of exhibiting the creative love which alone makes it possible for them to grow. Thus, the reality of community depends on the extent to which the individuals who make it up have become truly Christlike. No genuine community is possible without discipleship in this sense.

One would expect real community to develop inevitably from the efforts of individuals to follow Christ. If this is not in fact the case it can only be because the following of Christ has been misunderstood. It is not going apart to a desert place to pray. It is not focussing all one's attention on our heavenly Father. Christ did these things, but they are not the essential of his mission which was to save men, and which he fulfilled by *being* 'the love of God' (Rom. 8:39). To *be* the liberating power of love for others is the only authentic following of Christ, as it is the only real sharing in his mission.

SUFFERING

Father Moloney also notes that discipleship carries with it the obligation to suffer for Jesus, but unfortunately he does not deal with the point adequately. There is plenty of evidence in the gospels to support the thesis that a disciple must expect to suffer, and Paul considers suffering integral to the Christian life, but it is important to clarify what sort of suffering is in question.

The gospels speak of persecution due to the hatred of the world (Jn. 15:8), and such persecution appears as the sign of the true disciple. That they are not persecuted, therefore, should worry religious. The first Christians were persecuted because they were seen as a threat. Their bearing and conviction was an afront to accepted values. Their urgency pricked the bubble of the world's complacency. If religious are not persecuted it is because they are seen as harmless. The minute they attack the egocentric values of the world (as they should do, as Christ did) they become objects of hatred. This was clearly manifested in the civil rights movement in the United States. Regular church-going Catholics villified priests and sisters who dared to champion the cause of the negro. As long as they merely taught school and occupied themselves with church affairs they were ignored. It was only when they accepted the burden of the cross in attempting to transform the world that the gospel prophecies came true.

The genuine follower of Christ, therefore, must do more than merely be prepared to accept persecution if the occasion should arise. He must court opposition and abuse by loving enough to be inspired to change the world. This will mean taking unpopular stands. It will mean propagating ideas that society and some superiors judge unorthodox and dangerous. More fundamentally, however, it will mean developing a Christlike personality which makes it possible for those of good-will to accept the values of the gospel. Without this latter dimension words are powerless. 'If I speak in the tongues of men and of angels, but have not love, I am a noisy gong or a clanging cymbal' (1 Cor. 13:1). The true apostle, as opposed to the merely verbal liberal, must be prepared to say with Paul, 'Become imitators of me, as I am an imitator of Christ' (1 Cor. 11:1).

In addition to persecution stemming from those outside, the gospels also speak of 'taking up the cross', and 'dying to self' (e.g. Mt. 16:24-28). In the traditional teaching on the religious life these admonitions have been interpreted to mean that the religious should accept whatever was inflicted on him either by superiors or by circumstances. They were, and are, used as a cover-up for the most blatant mismanagement and lack of sensitivity. A refusal to accept a decision that is obviously silly and wrong is interpreted as a refusal of the cross, and any assertion of one's personality is interpreted as a refusal to die to oneself. The most perfect disciple of Christ is the religious who is most docile and passive. This is a complete distortion of the gospel message, as the teaching of Paul clearly shows.

The cross that the disciple must accept is the deep awareness of his inadequacy to fulfil the mission confided to him. He is so conscious of what he has received from God that he feels a terrible urgency to communicate the transforming power of Christ. As Paul says, 'If we are beside ourselves, it is for God. If we are in our right mind, it is for you. For the love of Christ constrains us' (2 Cor. 5:13-14). Yet the results are so meagre, and the true disciple will always look for the roots of failure in himself rather than in the blindness and obstinacy of others. In addition, there is the continuous adaptation necessary in order to meet individuals on their own level. 'To the weak I became weak, that I might win the weak. I have become all things to all men, that I might by all means save some' (1 Cor. 9:22). This is the real sacrifice of self which is intensified by the sympathy engendered by the bonds of love (Col. 3:14), 'Who is weak and I am not weak? Who is made to fall and I am not indignant?' (2 Cor. 11:29). The disciple must identify with those whom he desires to bring to Christ, 'Become as I am, because I became as you' (Gal. 4:12). Only in the process of this continuous active concern for others does the disciple acquire 'the mind of Christ' (1 Cor. 2:16) who emptied himself for us (Phil. 2:6-7). This is a painful process because it runs counter to the selfishness which is the deepest rooted of the inherited attitudes of sinful man, and no penances are necessary for one who fully accepts the responsibility of being Christ for others. Denials on the level of food, lodging, sleep, money, etc. are all irrelevant, and historically they were invented as substitutes for the crucifying concern that is the mark of the true follower of Christ. 'Bear one another's burdens, and so fulfil the law of Christ' (Gal. 6:2).

Suffering and sharing in the work of Christ, therefore, go hand in hand. One is not possible without the other. In that pain the disciple needs to be consoled. In that anguish he needs to be strengthened. In that weakness he needs to be uplifted. There must be others to bear *his* burden. He can only survive 'in Christ', that is, in a community whose members have truly 'put on Christ' (Gal. 3:27-28) in so far as they love and give themselves for each other (Gal. 2:20).